chocolate chip
cookies

CHOCOLATE CHIP COOKIES

DOZENS OF RECIPES FOR REINTERPRETED FAVORITES

by **Carey Jones & Robyn Lenzi**

Photographs by Antonis Achilleos

CHRONICLE BOOKS
SAN FRANCISCO

Library of Congress Cataloging-in-Publication Data available.

ISBN 978-1-4521-1168-1

Manufactured in China

MIX
Paper from
responsible sources
FSC® C008047

Designed by VANESSA DINA

Baking by CAREY JONES AND ROBYN LENZI

Surfaces by SFSURFACE.NET

Prop styling by SPORK

Illustrations by LYDIA ORTIZ

Typesetting by HOWIE SEVERSON

Nutella is a registered trademark of Ferrero USA, Inc.
Oreo Double Stuf is a registered trademark of Kraft Foods.
Maldon sea salt is a registered trademark of the Maldon Crystal Salt Co.

10 9 8 7 6 5 4 3 2 1

Chronicle Books LLC
680 Second Street
San Francisco, California 94107

WWW.CHRONICLEBOOKS.COM

Do you love chocolate chip cookies? Given that you're reading this book, we're guessing you do. You're not alone. While the chocolate chip cookie is the official dessert of both Massachusetts and Pennsylvania (who knew!?), it might as well be the signature cookie of every state: Americans eat an estimated seven billion chocolate chip cookies each year. And chocolate chip cookies make up half of all cookies baked in American households.

Chocolate chip cookies have long been a favorite go-to dessert and snack. As dessert trends come and go, chocolate chip cookies have always been a favorite, resistant to the passage of time and changing fashions and tastes. Chock-full of melty, gooey chocolate and brown-sugary buttery goodness, this cookie satisfies both chocolate lovers and cookie lovers, hitting that sweet spot (pun intended) right in the middle. It also provides a wonderful palette for experimentation: Add nuts, fruit, or other extras to a chocolate chip cookie, and it gets more interesting. Switch things up by using different flours, fats, and sweeteners, and the end result is still delicious. Chocolate chip cookies play nicely with other ingredients, too: Think a tall glass of cold milk for dunking, or a scoop of vanilla ice cream sandwiched by two chewy cookies. And on top of all that, chocolate chip cookies are portable and easy to make!

About This Book
We know that many store-bought chocolate chip cookies can hit the spot, but nothing beats the appeal of a homemade chocolate chip cookie, fresh out of the oven. That's where this book comes in. We want you to have more options than just the recipe on the back of the chocolate chip bag. Whether you're looking to add some novelty to your existing cookie repertoire, punch up your bake-sale offerings, or simply discover a new go-to chocolate chip recipe, you'll find it here.

An important thing you should know about us is that we are avowed fans of chocolate chip cookies. And that's a good thing, because while working on this book, we each ate about five hundred cookies (all in the name of research, of course). We've created what we believe to be forty-one of the tastiest chocolate chip cookies out there, and we want to share them with you.

First off, let's talk about what makes a chocolate chip cookie distinctive. Clearly, chocolate chips are the defining ingredient. But chocolate chip cookies also typically include a combination of brown sugar and white sugar, differentiating them from sugar cookies, which use only white sugar. The brown sugar adds caramelized notes and moisture. Both sugars are creamed together with butter, usually at room temperature, a process that helps the sugar dissolve more easily, for a smooth mouthfeel in the finished cookie. The butter also lends a rich taste and melts in the oven, allowing the cookie to spread. Eggs add richness and flavor to the dough and also act as a binding agent, holding the wet and dry ingredients together. Flour (usually all-purpose) provides the structure for the cookie. When wheat flour is mixed with other ingredients, gluten forms, giving the cookie its chewy texture. A leavener, typically baking soda, interacts with the moisture in the other ingredients and causes the dough to rise during baking. Baking soda also helps the cookie brown by reducing its acidity. Finally, a small amount of salt enhances the flavors in the cookie. While nuts, fruits, spices, and other additions are common in chocolate chip cookies, and we use them in many of our recipes, they aren't essential for a satisfying basic chocolate chip cookie. Finally, chocolate chip cookies are traditionally made as drop cookies, meaning they're portioned onto baking sheets, generally by the tablespoonful, and then the dough spreads out into round cookies during baking.

We've divided this book into six chapters, with the unifying theme being that every recipe contains chocolate in some form, whether chips, chunks, or chopped chocolate. Chapter 1: The Classics includes straight-up chocolate chip cookie recipes for those who like their cookies plain and simple—and, of course, delicious. After covering the basics, we move on to more creative cookies. Chapter 2: Not Just Chocolate Chips contains recipes with additions such as dried fruit, nuts, granola, and more, for people who like a chunkier cookie with more texture and flavor. Chapter 3: Savory Sweet capitalizes on the addictive quality of desserts with a hint of saltiness,

and offers cookies that have intriguing savory elements. Chapter 4: Alternative Ingredients contains recipes that utilize alternative flours and fats—perfect for those on restricted diets or who are simply interested in exploring new ingredients in baked goods. Chapter 5: Grown-Up Cookies offers recipes that are a bit more refined and sophisticated, such as bourbon-laced cookies, buttery shortbread studded with cacao nibs, and delicate wafer-like *tuiles*. Finally, the recipes in Chapter 6: Beyond Drop Cookies play with putting classic chocolate chip flavors into unexpected forms, such as cakes, bars, and even a cookie baked in a skillet.

Although the recipes in chapter 1 serve as inspiration for many of the other cookies in the book, they aren't base doughs for other recipes. Rather than simply adding mix-ins to the cookies in the later chapters, we formulated each recipe to make sure the flavors came together in the best possible way, then tested and retested to get each one just right. We do, however, encourage you to experiment with the recipes in the first chapter, adding whatever mix-ins you like.

When developing the recipes in this book, we wanted to make sure that the average home baker could pull them off with no problem. However, we also had some ambitious ideas, and to make them work a few of the recipes require slightly more complicated techniques. Where a recipe is a little trickier, or just takes a few more steps, we've noted it in the recipe.

One more note about the cookies in this book: In our experience, people tend to fall into one of three camps when it comes to cookie texture—crispy, soft, or chewy. Most of our recipes fall into one of those three categories, although a few do have different, unique textures. When relevant, we've noted whether the cookie is crispy, soft, or chewy to give you another benchmark when choosing what to bake.

Cookie Basics

Before we dive into the recipes, we want to address a few things so you can bake like a pro from the get-go. In addition to offering pointers on ingredients, we'll discuss measuring, mixing, resting dough, portioning cookies, freezing dough, baking, yields, and storage.

Ingredients

We believe that a cookie is only as good as the sum of its parts. And because a chocolate chip cookie has so few necessary parts—flour, sugar, butter, eggs, chocolate, salt, and leavener—we use the best-quality ingredients we can afford. We'll tell you what we prefer, but feel free to experiment and find the ingredients you love.

BAKING SODA AND BAKING POWDER

We aren't picky about leaveners—baking soda and baking powder. Any brand will do. However, it's important that you use leaveners that are fairly fresh. Over time, they lose their potency and won't provide adequate leavening, resulting in flat cookies.

Here are a couple of quick tests you can use to make sure your baking soda and powder are in tip-top shape:

FOR BAKING SODA: Put 1 to 2 tbsp of white vinegar in a small bowl and add 1 tsp of baking soda. If the soda bubbles and foams vigorously, you're good to go. If not, replace your box of baking soda.

FOR BAKING POWDER: Put 1 to 2 tbsp of warm tap water into a small bowl and add 1 tsp of baking powder. The mixture should fizz and form lots of tiny bubbles. If it doesn't, or if only a few bubbles form, buy new baking powder.

BUTTER

We always use unsalted butter in our cookies, as this allows us to control the amount of salt in the dough. In the United States, butter is graded either AA (highest quality), A, or B, and by law it must have at least 80 percent butterfat content. European and European-style butters are much richer, with butterfat content of 82 percent or higher. Compare one of these to your supermarket brand, and see if you can taste the difference. Our favorite brand of European-style butter is Plugrá.

We usually make cookie dough using butter at room temperature, which allows the

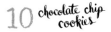

butter and sugar to cream together smoothly. Depending on the ambient temperature, butter that has been out of the fridge between one and four hours generally has the right consistency: soft to the touch but still retaining its shape. When recipes call for melted butter, you can melt butter straight out of the fridge, either in the microwave or in a saucepan on the stovetop.

CHOCOLATE

Because chocolate is the defining feature of chocolate chip cookies, we'll take a minute to explain how it's made. Cocoa beans (also known as cacao beans) are roasted and then winnowed to separate the shells from what's inside: pulp and nibs (pieces of the cocoa beans). The nibs are then ground into a paste known as chocolate liquor, which is sometimes further pressed to create two substances: cocoa powder and cocoa butter. The chocolate we know and love is created by mixing chocolate liquor and cocoa butter with sugar and massaging the mixture for hours or days in a process known as conching. Then the mixture is poured into molds to set.

Of course, chocolate comes in a variety of forms. In every recipe, we tell you what kind of chocolate to use. Many of the recipes use semisweet chocolate chips, which are traditional in chocolate chip cookies, but some use milk chocolate, some call for chopped chocolate, and others contain cacao nibs or cocoa powder. Here are brief descriptions of some of the most common forms of chocolate used in baking.

BAKING DISCS OR BAKING DROPS. Also known as discos, feves, pastilles, wafers, or callets, depending on the company that manufactures them, baking discs are made using the same types of chocolate available in bars and blocks. They don't have added emulsifiers, as chocolate chips do, and therefore are ideal for melting. When used in cookies in place of chocolate chips, they melt smoothly, creating layers of chocolate within the cookie. If you want to make a cookie that has chocolate in every bite, consider investing in a bag of baking discs.

BAR OR BLOCK CHOCOLATE. Bar chocolate contains fewer emulsifiers than chocolate chips and also tends to be of higher quality. Generally, the darker the chocolate, the more cocoa solids and the less sugar it contains.

BITTERSWEET CHOCOLATE. By law, bittersweet chocolate must contain at least 35 percent cocoa solids. Often it's much darker, with a cocoa content somewhere between 50 and 80 percent.

CACAO NIBS. As discussed, cacao nibs are a fairly unprocessed form of chocolate: basically just roasted, shelled cocoa beans separated from the pulp. They contain no sugar and have an intense, almost coffee-like taste and an addictive crunch.

CHOCOLATE CHIPS. To make chocolate chips, an emulsifier is added to the chocolate. This allows them to hold their shape while baking. Our favorite chocolate chips are Guittard brand. Because chocolate chips don't melt as well as bar chocolate, we recommend using bar chocolate or baking discs whenever you need to melt chocolate for a recipe.

CHOPPED CHOCOLATE. When chopping chocolate from a bar or block, we find it best to use a serrated knife. It grips the chocolate and helps prevent the knife from slipping. It's also helpful to work quickly so the chocolate doesn't melt from the warmth of your hands.

COCOA POWDER. Cocoa powder is the solid material extracted when cocoa butter is removed from cocoa beans. This mass is pulverized into powder, which can then be used for baking. There are two kinds of cocoa: natural and Dutch-process. Dutch-process cocoa has been treated with alkali for a smoother, milder taste, whereas natural cocoa has a sharper flavor. We use both in our recipes. Don't confuse cocoa powder with hot cocoa mix, which also contains sugar and other ingredients.

DARK CHOCOLATE. An umbrella term that encompasses both bittersweet and semisweet chocolate, "dark chocolate" can also refer to chocolate with a cocoa content less than 35 percent. The term is used to differentiate chocolate that contains no milk solids from milk chocolate.

MILK CHOCOLATE. Containing the least cocoa powder, milk chocolate also has powdered or condensed milk added. Therefore, it's lighter in color and in flavor than semisweet or bittersweet chocolate.

SEMISWEET CHOCOLATE. Also required to contain at least 35 percent cocoa solids, semisweet chocolate is generally sweeter than bittersweet, although the amount of sugar in bittersweet and semisweet chocolate is not regulated.

WHITE CHOCOLATE. Containing no cocoa solids at all, white chocolate is made from cocoa butter, sugar, and milk. We find it to be mostly sweet, with little character, so we don't use it.

EGGS

Our recipes call for large eggs, as opposed to small, medium, extra-large, or jumbo. Since many cookie recipes use just one egg, if you have a size other than large it usually won't make a difference in the finished recipe. However, for recipes that require more than one egg, it's best to use the correct size. Eggs can vary dramatically in size, and the difference in volume between three large eggs and three small eggs, for example, can throw off a recipe.

We also recommend bringing eggs to room temperature before baking cookies. This is especially important for recipes that have more eggs in them, like the whoopie pies (page 114) and madeleines (page 116). (Cold eggs may solidify room-temperature butter, preventing it from blending smoothly into the dough.) Just take them out of the fridge about an hour before you start mixing the dough. If you forget or are in a hurry, you can place cold eggs in a bowl of warm water for a few minutes to speed up the process.

FLOUR

The best type of flour for most cookies is high-quality unbleached all-purpose flour (we generally use King Arthur brand). However, you'll see that we sometimes call for different types of flour, such as whole-wheat flour, cake flour, or specialty flours such as quinoa or Kamut flour. Many of these flours are also available from King Arthur. For those that aren't, Bob's Red Mill brand is a good choice.

MILK

When we call for milk in our recipes, we mean whole milk. If you have only 2 percent, 1 percent, or skim milk on hand, those will work, too; they'll just give you a slightly less rich-tasting result.

A couple of our recipes call for small amounts of buttermilk. While you can buy buttermilk at the grocery store, it's quick and simple to make your own, and if you don't have other uses for buttermilk, making your own may be the best bet when you need a small quantity. Simply add about ¾ teaspoon of white vinegar or lemon juice to ¼ cup of milk, stir once or twice, and let sit at room temperature until the milk thickens slightly, about 10 minutes.

NUTS

We use raw, unsalted nuts in our recipes unless otherwise specified. Store nuts in the freezer to preserve freshness; the oil in nuts gives them a limited shelf life at room temperature. Nuts can be chopped either by hand or in the food processor. To toast nuts, preheat the oven to 350°F/180°C/gas mark 4. Spread the nuts evenly on a rimmed baking sheet and toast in the center of the oven for 10 minutes, until golden and fragrant. Let cool before chopping.

SALT

We use kosher salt (Diamond Crystal brand, to be precise) in all our recipes unless otherwise specified. Kosher salt is considered a coarse salt. You can substitute table salt, iodized salt, or sea salt, but be aware whether you are using fine or coarse. Use about 25 percent less if you substitute fine salt for coarse salt.

SUGAR

As discussed, one quality that characterizes the typical chocolate chip cookie is a combination of granulated and brown sugars, and most recipes in this book include both.

GRANULATED SUGAR. We use white granulated cane sugar from C&H (which stands for California and Hawaiian Sugar Company), but any brand of granulated cane sugar will work just fine.

BROWN SUGAR. We prefer dark brown sugar, rather than light brown sugar or golden brown sugar. It has a higher molasses content, and its more distinctive caramel flavors work nicely in chocolate chip cookies. However, if you have another type of brown sugar on hand, it will do.

VANILLA
We use pure vanilla extract, never imitation.

ZEST
We think zest (the colored part of the peel of lemons, limes, oranges, and other citrus fruits) is a powerful and underutilized ingredient in baking. It's full of volatile essential oils that give great flavor and aroma to a finished cookie. We use a Microplane zester, which creates fluffy, fine shavings of the peel without picking up any of the bitter white pith, and we encourage you to do the same.

Measuring Ingredients
In this book, we list dry ingredients by volume (in cups) as well as by weight (in grams). Wet ingredients are listed by volume (in cups and milliliters).

We're here to tell you that a digital kitchen scale is your friend. Digital scales are inexpensive and widely available, including online. Professional bakers do all their measuring by weight, and for good reason. We've found it to be the best way to get consistent results. Plus, it's easier. No more scooping and sweeping or wondering if nuts should be chopped before or after measuring.

If you don't have a digital scale or prefer to measure by volume, we have some tips on how best to do that. Rather than burying your measuring cup in the flour or sugar sack and scooping out what you need, we recommend that you scoop from the sack with a large spoon and gently tip the spoon's contents into the measuring cup. Repeat until the cup is full, and then run the spoon handle across the top of the cup to level it off. The only thing this doesn't hold true for is brown sugar, which should be firmly packed into a measuring cup or measuring spoon.

To measure wet ingredients, use measuring cups specifically designed for liquids, as they tend to be more accurate for these ingredients. To ensure you've measured the correct amount, get down so the volume markers on the side of the cup are at eye level.

For smaller measurements (teaspoons and tablespoons), any type of measuring spoons work equally well for wet and dry ingredients.

In a few recipes, we call for sifting the dry ingredients before combining them with the wet ingredients. Sifting lightens dry ingredients, adding volume. It also breaks up clumps.

When a recipe calls for sifting, measure the ingredients out first (using the scoop-and-level method), and then sift them. You can use an actual sifter, with a handle that turns to work the ingredients through the sieve, or use a fine-meshed sieve or strainer. Simply pour the dry ingredients into the sieve and tap the side of the sieve with your hand until all the contents are sifted.

Mixing Ingredients

For the most part, the ingredients for our cookie recipes can be combined by hand using a wooden spoon or stiff spatula, in a stand mixer, or with a handheld mixer. We prefer to use a stand mixer; it does most of the work, and makes the process much faster. However, the cookies will turn out equally well if you mix by hand or with a handheld mixer. Whichever method you choose, the key is to avoid overmixing, which can develop too much gluten in the flour, leading to tough cookies. (Feel free to insert your own "tough cookie" pun here.) Therefore, once you combine the wet and dry ingredients, we recommend mixing just until they are combined, meaning as soon as you can no longer see streaks of flour in the dough.

The doughs in this book vary greatly in appearance and texture. Typical chocolate chip cookie dough is smooth, dense, and somewhat pliable. However, some of the doughs in this book are very thick, crumbly, and almost dry, while others are quite wet and thin. We describe the optimum consistency in each recipe so you'll know what to aim for.

Resting Dough

A secret trick of cookie experts is to rest the dough before baking, covering and refrigerating it for twelve to twenty-four hours before portioning. Resting cookie dough allows the ingredients to coalesce and meld together and can improve flavor. We've found that allowing dough to rest overnight in the fridge does indeed result in a deeper flavor, and that it also helps cookies hold their shape during baking. All the recipes in this book call for baking immediately after mixing, but about half of them will benefit from resting the dough if you have the time, and when that's the case, we've noted it in the recipe. In general, cookies that don't do well with resting are either not drop cookies or include crunchy or crispy mix-ins or alternative fats or flours.

Portioning Cookies

Portioning out even amounts of dough onto baking sheets will help ensure that the cookies bake evenly. We've found that, in most cases, a rounded tablespoon of dough makes a nice-size cookie—not too big and not too small. We use a handy scoop called the Zeroll Universal EZ Disher (size 40). It's shaped like a mini ice-cream scoop, holds about 1½ tablespoons, and makes it a cinch to drop balls of dough quickly onto baking sheets. You can buy these scoops—made by Zeroll or other manufacturers—online or at kitchen stores. Alternatively, just use a well-rounded tablespoon measure to portion out your dough. Your cookies may not be as perfectly circular, but they will be perfectly delicious!

If you like mini cookies or giant cookies, we recommend that you portion out just a few and bake them as a test batch before proceeding. Most of the drop cookies in this book can be made in different sizes as long as you adjust the baking time accordingly. Mini cookies should bake for a shorter amount of time than the recipe calls for, and extra-large cookies should bake longer. Baked goods that require special treatment or different vessels for baking—like the shortbread and other recipes at the end of chapter 5 and all the recipes in chapter 6—should be made only as specified in the recipe.

Freezing Dough

With most of the recipes in this book, it's okay to freeze cookie dough and bake it later. In the few cases where this doesn't work well, we've noted that in the recipe. To freeze cookie dough, portion it onto a parchment-lined baking sheet. You can put the dough balls quite close together since they won't be baked. Then wrap the baking sheet in plastic wrap and freeze for about an hour. Once the dough is frozen, remove the baking sheet from the freezer and transfer the frozen balls to a large zip-top bag. Return them to the freezer, where they will remain in good condition for up to two months. Thaw before baking, either at room temperature until the dough is pliable, or in the fridge overnight. Be aware that the colder the dough is, the less it will spread in the oven.

Baking Tips

Making a delicious cookie dough is only half the battle—next you need to bake it. We have some tips and tricks that will help ensure your cookies are baked to perfection.

If there's just one thing we want you to take away from this section, it's that the type of baking sheet used has a substantial impact on the finished product. Most baking sheets are made of thin, dark-colored aluminum. The thin metal can warp in the oven and the dark surface absorbs heat quickly, often leading to cookies that are burned on the bottom—not good! We recommend that you invest in a few commercial-grade baking sheets (also called jelly-roll pans or half-size sheet pans). Look for sheets with a 1-in/2.5-cm rim on all sides that are heavy, light silver in color, and free of nonstick coating. They are a little more expensive, but they're worth it. They will last forever, and we promise that they will yield superior results. Chicago Metallic seems to be the most popular U.S. brand, but there are others.

We generally bake our cookies on silicone baking mats that nestle inside baking sheets. They're nonstick, so cookies slide right off, and the sheets can be washed and reused for years. We prefer Silpat brand.

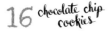

Lining baking sheets with parchment paper is, in our view, the next best bet. Coating a bare baking sheet or one lined with a sheet of aluminum foil with a light coating of canola-oil-based cooking spray (such as Pam) will also work in a pinch, but we really recommend using silicone baking mats or parchment. For the recipes where it makes a true difference, we've noted it.

You may be surprised to learn that the actual temperatures in your oven can vary considerably from the setting you select. We recommend using an oven thermometer for the best accuracy. We have also included a two-minute range of baking times for each recipe (for example, "bake for 13 to 15 minutes") to account for inaccurate oven temperatures, as well as a visual cue for how each finished recipe should look.

Since cookies are fairly small and bake quickly, you can bake two sheets at once. We recommend positioning the racks so they divide the oven into thirds. In other words, place two oven racks so that they're evenly spaced, one a third of the distance from the top of the oven and the other a third of the way from the bottom. Remove any extra oven racks. Halfway through the baking time, rotate the baking sheets, moving the top one to the bottom shelf and vice versa, and also turning the sheets so the part of the sheet that was in the back of the oven is in the front. This will ensure more even baking, especially if there are any hot spots in your oven.

If you bake only one sheet of cookies at a time—for example, if you're making a half batch—keep in mind that a single sheet of cookies will bake more quickly than two sheets. Therefore, you should use the lower end of the range of baking times. You should also focus more on the description of how the cookies should look and feel when they are fully baked in this case.

If you have access to a convection oven, consider yourself lucky. It will make for speedier and more efficient cookie baking. Convection ovens have fans that circulate heat throughout the oven, providing an even baking temperature throughout, along with faster cooking times. If you use a convection oven, we recommend reducing the baking temperature by 25°F/15°C. Also note that the baking time will probably be on the lower end of the range indicated in the recipe.

Yields

The recipes in this book generally yield between two and three dozen cookies. All the recipes can be halved or doubled with no adjustments to the method. In a few recipes, nuts are optional. In those cases the yield is based on not including the nuts.

Storage

After baked cookies have cooled completely, store them in an airtight container at room temperature. Most will remain fresh for two to three days. And if a batch of cookies isn't eaten within three days, you have stronger willpower than we do.

The Science behind the Cookie

Cookies are a fascinating science experiment. As mentioned, this book includes cookies with a variety of textures, from crispy to soft to chewy. We've formulated the recipes in ways that we think work well. Still, you may want to tweak the recipes to suit your tastes. For example, if you're a die-hard fan of chewy cookies and want to experiment with a crispy or soft cookie recipe to make it more chewy, be our guest! We've found that a few slight adjustments can help create the desired texture. So before we move on to the recipes, let's take a look at the science of cookie textures.

Adjustments for Crispier Cookies

If you want to make crispier cookies, try adjusting the ingredients or method in the following ways.

FLOUR: Use less flour for more spread.

BUTTER: Melt the butter instead of using butter at room temperature. (Wait until it has cooled slightly before combining it with other ingredients.)

SUGAR: Use a higher ratio of white sugar to brown sugar.

MIXING: Be extra careful not to overmix the dough.

PORTIONING: Flatten the dough balls before baking the cookies.

BAKING: Bake at a slightly higher temperature, and bake until the cookies are uniformly golden, not just golden around the edges.

Adjustments for Softer Cookies

If you want to make softer cookies, try adjusting the ingredients or method in the following ways.

FLOUR: Use a higher-protein flour, such as bread flour. (This is especially helpful if you add an egg yolk, as recommended below, helping hold the wetter dough together.)

SUGAR: Use a higher ratio of brown sugar to white sugar.

EGGS: Add an egg yolk, which will create a dough with a higher ratio of fat and moisture.

MIXING: Cream the butter and sugars thoroughly for extra softness and lightness. Rest the dough to allow the flour to absorb more moisture.

BAKING: Take care not to overbake, as this will result in harder cookies.

Adjustments for Chewier Cookies

If you want to make chewier cookies, try adjusting the ingredients or method in the following ways.

FLOUR: Use more flour for less spread and added density. Using bread flour can also be helpful.

 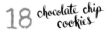

BUTTER: Use less butter for less spread.

EGGS: Use less egg (which means less liquid) for a higher proportion of dry to wet ingredients.

MIXING: Be sure to mix the dough well. Resting the dough will allow the larger ratio of flour to be more fully coated with other ingredients.

BAKING: Start baking at a higher temperature to set the crusty exterior, then lower the temperature to finish baking the cookies evenly without burning the edges.

While researching this book, we discovered many articles and blog posts dedicated to the quest for the perfect or ultimate chocolate chip cookie. We believe that it simply isn't possible to make a perfect chocolate chip cookie that works for everyone; there are just too many variations in individual preferences. But we do hope that in one of these forty-one recipes, you'll discover your own personal perfect chocolate chip cookie. Happy baking!

CHAPTER 1: **The Classics**

This chapter gives you the basics: straight-up chocolate chip cookie recipes without much adornment. These cookies serve as base recipes for several other cookies in the book, so this is a great place for you to get your cookie-baking feet wet. Whether you prefer crispy, soft, or chewy cookies, you'll find a reliable recipe here. For each, we'll also give you our reasoning behind why we used the quantities and forms of ingredients we did, and how they combine to make the tastiest cookie possible.

Crispy 22

Soft 25

Chewy 26

Triple-
Chocolate 28

CRISPY

1 cup/125 g unbleached all-purpose flour

¼ tsp baking soda

½ tsp salt

½ cup/115 g unsalted butter

⅔ cup/130 g granulated sugar

⅓ cup/65 g packed dark brown sugar

1 egg

1 tsp pure vanilla extract

1 cup/170 g finely chopped semisweet chocolate (55 to 65% cocoa)

1 cup/115 g finely chopped pecans, walnuts, or almonds (optional)

We are both big fans of crispy cookies, so we were especially excited to develop this recipe. (Don't worry, chewy cookie fans, we have recipes for you, too.) This cookie is thin, almost wafer-like, and has a satisfying crunch surrounding small morsels of nuts and chocolate. It's buttery without being greasy and has caramelized undertones that keep you coming back for more.

The melted butter and relatively small amount of flour ensure a flat, thin cookie, while a lower ratio of brown sugar to white sugar keeps the cookie crunchy. Finally, we use chopped chocolate because it doesn't overwhelm the cookie the way chips might.

Preheat the oven to 375°F/190°C/gas mark 5. Adjust the racks so they divide the oven into thirds. Line two baking sheets with parchment paper.

Whisk together the flour, baking soda, and salt in a medium bowl.

Melt the butter in a small saucepan on the stove or in a microwave-safe container in the microwave. Let cool until just barely warm to the touch.

Transfer the butter to a stand mixer fitted with the paddle attachment and add both sugars. Mix on medium speed until well blended, about 30 seconds. Add the egg and vanilla and mix until completely combined. Scrape the sides of the bowl with a spatula. Add the flour mixture and mix on low speed until just combined, scraping the bowl if necessary to incorporate the dry ingredients. Add the chopped chocolate and nuts (if using) and mix on low speed until evenly distributed. The dough should be slightly shiny and loose. (This dough benefits from resting for 12 to 24 hours before baking.)

Using a small ice-cream scoop or tablespoon measure, drop well-rounded balls of dough onto the prepared baking sheets about 2 in/5 cm apart. Dampen the palm of your hand and flatten each cookie until about ¼ in/6 mm thick.

Bake for 14 to 16 minutes, rotating the baking sheets halfway through the baking time, until the cookies are evenly golden. It is important to bake the cookies fully to ensure crispness throughout.

When cool enough to handle, transfer to wire racks to cool completely. The cookies will get crisper as they cool. Stored in an airtight container at room temperature, the cookies will keep for 2 to 3 days.

SOFT

Like the crispy cookie (page 22), this one is on the thin side, but it has a soft chewiness to it. It reminds us of the Keebler Soft Batch or Mrs. Fields cookies we loved as kids, but made with only pure, high-quality ingredients.

Bread flour, with its high gluten content, gives the cookie its soft bite, and an extra egg yolk helps bind the dough. It has a high percentage of brown sugar to white sugar, resulting in a deeper, more caramelized flavor.

Preheat the oven to 350°F/180°C/gas mark 4. Adjust the racks so they divide the oven into thirds. Line two baking sheets with parchment paper.

Whisk together the flour, baking soda, and salt in a medium bowl.

In a stand mixer fitted with the paddle attachment, cream the butter and both sugars on medium speed until smooth and well blended, about 1 minute. Add the egg and mix until completely combined. Add the egg yolk and vanilla and mix until completely combined. Scrape the sides of the bowl with a spatula. Add the flour mixture and mix on low speed until just combined, scraping the bowl if necessary to incorporate the dry ingredients. Add the chocolate chips and nuts (if using) and mix on low speed until evenly distributed. The dough should be smooth, dense, and somewhat pliable. (This dough benefits from resting in the fridge, covered, for 12 to 24 hours before baking.)

Using a small ice-cream scoop or tablespoon measure, drop well-rounded balls of dough onto the prepared baking sheets about 2 in/5 cm apart.

Bake for 12 to 14 minutes, rotating the baking sheets halfway through the baking time, just until the edges turn golden.

When cool enough to handle, transfer to wire racks to cool completely. Stored in an airtight container at room temperature, the cookies will keep for 2 to 3 days.

MAKES ABOUT 27 COOKIES

1¼ cups/155 g unbleached bread flour

¼ tsp baking soda

¼ tsp salt

½ cup/115 g unsalted butter, at room temperature

¼ cup/50 g granulated sugar

¾ cup plus 1 tbsp/160 g packed dark brown sugar

1 egg

1 egg yolk

½ tsp pure vanilla extract

¾ cup/125 g semisweet chocolate chips

¾ cup/85 g chopped nuts (optional)

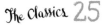

CHEWY

MAKES ABOUT 36 COOKIES

2¼ cups/280 g unbleached
all-purpose flour

½ tsp baking soda

½ tsp salt

½ cup/115 g unsalted
butter, at room temperature

¾ cup/150 g granulated
sugar

½ cup/100 g packed dark
brown sugar

1 egg

½ tsp pure vanilla extract

⅔ cup/115 g semisweet
chocolate chips

⅔ cup/75 g chopped nuts
(optional)

This recipe existed long before we started putting this book together. Many years ago, Robyn tasted a thick and chewy chocolate chip cookie that she loved and then spent many hours trying to reverse engineer it, finally coming up with this recipe. (Ironically, after we developed the crispy cookie recipe, Robyn switched camps and now favors that type.)

The dough for this cookie is on the dry side, which gives the finished product a denser, more toothsome chew. It also has a higher ratio of white sugar to brown sugar, resulting in a milder flavor. While this cookie is delicious on its own, it also stands up well to a lot of additions—nuts, dried fruit, coconut, and more. So if you're a fan of chunky cookies, feel free to throw in your favorite additions to make this recipe your own.

Preheat the oven to 400°F/200°C/gas mark 6. Adjust the racks so they divide the oven into thirds. Line two baking sheets with parchment paper.

Whisk together the flour, baking soda, and salt in a medium bowl.

In a stand mixer fitted with the paddle attachment, cream the butter and both sugars on medium speed until smooth and well blended, about 1 minute. Add the egg and vanilla and mix until completely combined. Scrape the sides of the bowl with a spatula. Add the flour mixture and mix on low speed until just combined, scraping the bowl if necessary to incorporate the dry ingredients. Add the chocolate chips and nuts (if using) and mix on low speed until evenly distributed. The dough should be somewhat dry and almost crumbly. (This dough benefits from resting in the fridge, covered, for 12 to 24 hours before baking.)

Using a small ice-cream scoop or tablespoon measure, drop well-rounded balls of dough onto the prepared baking sheets about 2 in/5 cm apart. Dampen the palm of your hand and flatten each cookie until about ¾ in/2 cm thick.

Put the baking sheets in the oven and immediately decrease the temperature to 300°F/150°C/gas mark 2. Bake for 17 to 20 minutes, rotating the baking sheets halfway through the baking time, just until the edges turn golden.

When cool enough to handle, transfer to wire racks to cool completely. Stored in an airtight container at room temperature, the cookies will keep for to 2 to 3 days.

 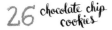

TRIPLE-CHOCOLATE

MAKES ABOUT 26 COOKIES

¾ cup plus 2 tbsp/105 g
unbleached bread flour

2 tbsp Dutch-process cocoa
powder

½ tsp baking soda

½ tsp salt

⅔ cup/115 g chopped semi-
sweet chocolate (approxi-
mately 58% cocoa)

6 tbsp/85 g unsalted
butter, at room temperature

½ cup/100 g granulated
sugar

¼ cup/50 g packed dark
brown sugar

2 eggs

1 tsp pure vanilla extract

1 cup/170 g semisweet
chocolate chips

1 cup/115 g chopped nuts
(optional)

If you don't think a classic chocolate chip cookie has nearly enough chocolate in it, this is the cookie for you. We wanted to make this cookie super-rich, so we used not just one kind of chocolate, but three: cocoa powder, melted semisweet chocolate, and chocolate chips. Because we used both butter and melted chocolate, which decrease the development of the gluten, we needed a strong flour to hold the cookie together. We chose bread flour, which is higher in protein, to provide more gluten strength.

We prefer Dutch-process cocoa here, which is treated with alkali, making it less acidic and softer in flavor than regular cocoa powder. However, regular cocoa powder, also called natural cocoa powder, will work just fine if that's what you have on hand.

This cookie is thinner and flatter than most of the cookies in this book because of all the chocolate and has a slight chew that we find irresistible. Add nuts, if you like, to balance the chocolate and for more textural contrast.

Preheat the oven to 350°F/180°C/gas mark 4. Adjust the racks so they divide the oven into thirds. Line two baking sheets with parchment paper.

Whisk together the flour, cocoa powder, baking soda, and salt in a medium bowl.

Using either a double boiler or microwave (see Cook's Note, page 30), melt the chopped chocolate in a small bowl. Keep warm.

In a stand mixer fitted with the paddle attachment, cream the butter and both sugars on medium speed until smooth and well blended, about 1 minute. Add the eggs and vanilla and mix until completely combined. Scrape the sides of the bowl with a spatula. Add the melted chocolate and mix until completely combined. Add the flour mixture and mix on low speed until just combined, scraping the bowl if necessary to incorporate the dry ingredients. Add the chocolate chips and nuts (if using) and mix on low speed until evenly distrib-uted. The dough should be sticky and on the thin side. (This dough benefits from resting in the fridge, covered, for 12 to 24 hours before baking.)

Using a small ice-cream scoop or tablespoon measure, drop well-rounded balls of dough onto the prepared baking sheets about 2 in/5 cm apart.

cont'd

Bake for 9 to 11 minutes, rotating the baking sheets halfway through the baking time, until the edges firm up slightly and the centers are no longer shiny.

When cool enough to handle, transfer to wire racks to cool completely. Stored in an airtight container at room temperature, the cookies will keep for 2 to 3 days.

Cook's Note

Melting chocolate using the double boiler method: If you have a double boiler, you're probably familiar with how to use it. If you don't, you can improvise a double boiler by putting the chocolate in a metal or glass bowl set over a pan of simmering water and stirring until the chocolate is melted and smooth.

Melting chocolate using the microwave method: To melt chocolate in a microwave, put it in a microwave-safe bowl and cook on high heat for 30-second intervals, taking the bowl out and stirring the chocolate after each interval until melted.

HISTORY OF THE
CHOCOLATE CHIP COOKIE

The chocolate chip cookie was created in the 1930s by Ruth Graves Wakefield, an owner of the Toll House Inn in Whitman, Massachusetts. As the story goes, she was baking a batch of chocolate cookies and realized she had run out of baking chocolate. As a substitute, she chopped up semisweet chocolate and stirred it into the dough, expecting it to melt into the cookies upon baking. When that didn't happen, the first chocolate chip cookie was born.

Others (including descendants of Wakefield's coworkers at the inn) dispute this account, claiming that Wakefield was a knowledgable baker and would have known enough about the properties of chocolate to understand that chopped-up chocolate wouldn't melt completely as the cookies baked. According to their story, a bar of semisweet chocolate fell from a shelf above Wakefield's work station into her industrial mixer as she was making a batch of her renowned Butter Drop Do sugar cookies. The chocolate was broken into chunks by the electric mixer, and rather than throw out the amended dough, Wakefield and her fellow bakers decided to bake it.

However it came about, the happy accident that created the chocolate chip cookie proved a boon for Wakefield. She dubbed her creation the Toll House Chocolate Crunch Cookie, and it became an instant hit with her customers. She eventually published it in local newspapers, and then in a cookbook that was distributed nationwide. It's rumored that she sold the recipe and the name to Nestlé in exchange for a lifetime supply of their chocolate. Henceforth, the recipe has appeared on the back of every bag of their semisweet chocolate morsels, probably making Toll House cookies the most-baked cookie in the United States.

CHAPTER 2: **Not Just Chocolate Chips**

If you like cookies with more flavors or textures, this is the chapter for you. Read on for recipes that include delicious combinations of mix-ins, beyond the basic chocolate chips and nuts. Some of these cookies are more familiar, such as a chocolate chip take on classic oatmeal-raisin cookies (page 41) and cookies enhanced with macadamia nuts (page 37). Others have unusual twists, containing ingredients such as honey and pistachios (page 48) or coconut and sesame seeds (page 46). And to take things over the top, we've even included a recipe that uses Oreo cookies as an ingredient (page 50).

Malted Hazelnut-Chocolate 34

Dark Chocolate-Macadamia 37

German Chocolate 38

Oatmeal-Raisin 41

Granola & Chocolate 44

Coconut-Sesame 46

Honey-Pistachio 48

A Cookie within a Cookie: The "Deconstructed" Oreo 50

MALTED HAZELNUT-CHOCOLATE

MAKES ABOUT 30 COOKIES

1¼ cups plus 2 tbsp/170 g unbleached all-purpose flour

¼ cup/30 g malted milk powder

½ tsp baking soda

½ tsp salt

½ cup/115 g unsalted butter, at room temperature

¼ cup/50 g granulated sugar

¾ cup plus 2 tbsp/175 g packed dark brown sugar

⅔ cup/200 g hazelnut-chocolate spread, such as Nutella

1 egg

1 tsp pure vanilla extract

⅔ cup/115 g semisweet chocolate chips

⅔ cup/75 g hazelnuts, toasted, skinned (see Cook's Note, page 36), and chopped

We're fond of Nutella brand hazelnut-chocolate spread and couldn't resist the idea of incorporating it in a chocolate chip cookie. This recipe also includes malted milk powder. We found that the warm, yeasty flavor of the malt complements the hazelnut-chocolate spread wonderfully. Chopped hazelnuts intensify the nuttiness of the cookie, and chocolate chips provide little bursts of sweetness.

Preheat the oven to 350°F/180°C/gas mark 4. Adjust the racks so they divide the oven into thirds. Line two baking sheets with parchment paper.

Whisk together the flour, malted milk powder, baking soda, and salt in a medium bowl.

In a stand mixer fitted with the paddle attachment, cream the butter and both sugars on medium speed until smooth and well blended, about 1 minute. Add the hazelnut-chocolate spread and mix until completely combined. Add the egg and vanilla and mix until completely combined. Scrape the sides of the bowl with a spatula. Add the flour mixture and mix on low speed until just combined, scraping the bowl if necessary to incorporate the dry ingredients. Add the chocolate chips and hazelnuts and mix on low speed until evenly distributed. The dough should look a little smoother than typical chocolate chip cookie dough because of the addition of the hazelnut-chocolate spread.

Using a small ice-cream scoop or tablespoon measure, drop well-rounded balls of dough onto the prepared baking sheets about 2 in/5 cm apart.

Bake for 13 to 15 minutes, rotating the baking sheets halfway through the baking time, until no longer shiny but still soft in the center.

When cool enough to handle, transfer to wire racks to cool completely. Stored in an airtight container at room temperature, the cookies will keep for 2 to 3 days.

Cook's Note

To skin hazelnuts, preheat the oven to 350°F/180°C/gas mark 4. Put the hazelnuts on a rimmed baking sheet and bake for 10 minutes, until fragrant. Remove them from the oven and pour them onto a large, clean kitchen towel. Gather up the edges of the towel, enclosing the hazelnuts, and rub vigorously between your hands. The friction will remove the skins. It's not necessary to remove every bit of skin; hazelnuts are notoriously difficult to skin completely.

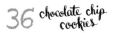

DARK CHOCOLATE—MACADAMIA

We know a lot of people like cookies with white chocolate and macadamia nuts, but to our tastes white chocolate is cloyingly sweet, macadamia nuts are on the oily side, and such cookies are, on the whole, fairly one-dimensional. In this recipe, we use bittersweet chocolate rather than white chocolate, and the macadamia nuts are ground up, not whole. The result is a cookie with a more complex flavor. Even if you like the more traditional version, give this one a try. You may become a convert!

Preheat the oven to 350°F/180°C/gas mark 4. Adjust the racks so they divide the oven into thirds. Line two baking sheets with parchment paper.

Whisk together the flour, baking soda, and salt in a medium bowl.

In a food processor, pulse the macadamia nuts until finely chopped, being careful not to process them too long, which would create a paste.

In a stand mixer fitted with the paddle attachment, cream the butter and both sugars on medium speed until well blended, about 1 minute. Add the egg and vanilla and mix until completely combined. Scrape the sides of the bowl with a spatula. Add the flour mixture and mix on low speed until just combined, scraping the bowl if necessary to incorporate the dry ingredients. Add the macadamia nuts and chocolate and mix on low speed until evenly distributed. The dough should be soft and a little sticky. (This dough benefits from resting in the fridge, covered, for 12 to 24 hours before baking.)

Using a small ice-cream scoop or tablespoon measure, drop well-rounded balls of dough onto the prepared baking sheets about 2 in/5 cm apart.

Bake for 9 to 11 minutes, rotating the baking sheets halfway through the baking time, just until the edges turn golden.

When cool enough to handle, transfer to wire racks to cool completely. Stored in an airtight container at room temperature, the cookies will keep for 2 to 3 days.

MAKES ABOUT 24 COOKIES

1½ cups/185 g unbleached all-purpose flour

½ tsp baking soda

½ tsp salt

½ cup/65 g macadamia nuts

½ cup/115 g unsalted butter, at room temperature

½ cup/100 g granulated sugar

⅔ cup/130 g packed dark brown sugar

1 egg

½ tsp pure vanilla extract

⅔ cup/115 g chopped bittersweet chocolate (65 to 72% cocoa)

Chewy

GERMAN CHOCOLATE

MAKES ABOUT 24 COOKIES

Filling

2½ tbsp milk

1 tbsp unsalted butter, melted

2 tsp egg yolk

2 tbsp granulated sugar

Pinch of salt

¼ cup/30 g pecans, toasted and chopped (toasting is optional)

6 tbsp/35 g unsweetened shredded dried coconut

cont'd

We love the combination of pecans, coconut, and chocolate that characterizes German chocolate cake. This cookie incorporates those same ingredients in an innovative way. The cookie has a rich coconut-pecan surprise hidden inside, providing a textural contrast and a burst of coconut sweetness.

The coconut-pecan filling makes enough for two batches of cookies, so if you want to make a double batch of cookies, you won't need to double the filling.

Make the filling. Line a large plate or small baking sheet with parchment paper. In a small saucepan, combine the milk, butter, egg yolk, sugar, salt, pecans, and coconut and cook over medium-low heat, stirring constantly with a heatproof spatula, until the mixture thickens, 5 to 7 minutes. Transfer to a small bowl. Using a teaspoon or tiny scoop, portion 24 rounded teaspoons of the mixture onto the parchment-lined plate. Freeze for 15 minutes.

Preheat the oven to 350°F/180°C/gas mark 4. Adjust the racks so they divide the oven into thirds. Line two baking sheets with parchment paper.

Whisk together the flour, baking soda, and salt in a medium bowl.

In a stand mixer fitted with the paddle attachment, cream the butter and both sugars on medium speed until smooth and well blended, about 1 minute. Add the egg and mix until completely combined. Add the milk and vanilla and mix until completely combined. Scrape the sides of the bowl with a spatula. Add the flour mixture and mix on low speed until just combined, scraping the bowl if necessary to incorporate the dry ingredients. Add the chocolate chips and mix on low speed until evenly distributed. The dough should be sticky. (This dough benefits from resting in the fridge, covered, for 12 to 24 hours before baking.)

Using a small ice-cream scoop or tablespoon measure, scoop out well-rounded balls of dough. Make a hollow in each ball of dough with your thumb and push a ball of filling into the hollow. Close the dough around the filling, adding a bit more dough if necessary to enclose it completely. Place the balls of dough on the prepared baking sheets, seam-side down, about 2 in/5 cm apart.

cont'd

2¼ cups/280 g unbleached all-purpose flour

½ tsp baking soda

½ tsp salt

½ cup/115 g unsalted butter, at room temperature

1 cup plus 2 tbsp/225 g granulated sugar

⅓ cup/65 g packed dark brown sugar

1 egg

¼ cup/60 ml milk

½ tsp pure vanilla extract

⅔ cup/115 g semisweet chocolate chips

Bake for 12 to 14 minutes, rotating the baking sheets halfway through the baking time, until evenly golden.

When cool enough to handle, transfer to wire racks to cool completely. Stored in an airtight container at room temperature, the cookies will keep for 2 to 3 days.

OATMEAL-RAISIN

Oatmeal-raisin is a classic in the cookie canon and chocolate-covered raisins are a popular snack, so we figured a cookie with oatmeal, raisins, and chocolate chips was bound to be a winner. Since oats have a naturally mild taste, we've boosted their flavor in this cookie by using whole-wheat flour, maple syrup, and a higher proportion of brown sugar.

Preheat the oven to 325°F/165°C/gas mark 3. Adjust the racks so they divide the oven into thirds. Line two baking sheets with parchment paper.

Whisk together both flours, the baking soda, and salt in a medium bowl.

In a stand mixer fitted with the paddle attachment, cream the butter and both sugars on medium speed until smooth and well blended, about 1 minute. Add the egg and mix until completely combined. Add the maple syrup and vanilla and mix until completely combined. Scrape the sides of the bowl with a spatula. Add the flour mixture and mix on low speed until just combined, scraping the bowl if necessary to incorporate the dry ingredients. Add the oats and mix on low speed just until combined. Add the chocolate chips and raisins and mix on low speed until evenly distributed. The dough should be very thick. (This dough benefits from resting in the fridge, covered, for 12 to 24 hours before baking.)

Using a small ice-cream scoop or tablespoon measure, drop well-rounded balls of dough onto the prepared baking sheets about 2 in/5 cm apart.

Bake for 14 to 16 minutes, rotating the baking sheets halfway through the baking time, just until the edges turn golden.

When cool enough to handle, transfer to wire racks to cool completely. Stored in an airtight container at room temperature, the cookies will keep for 2 to 3 days.

MAKES ABOUT 32 COOKIES

¾ cup plus 2 tbsp/105 g unbleached all-purpose flour

6 tbsp/45 g whole-wheat flour

½ tsp baking soda

1 tsp salt

5 tbsp/70 g unsalted butter, at room temperature

¼ cup/50 g granulated sugar

¾ cup/150 g packed dark brown sugar

1 egg

¼ cup/60 ml pure maple syrup

1 tsp pure vanilla extract

1½ cups/125 g old-fashioned rolled oats (not instant)

1 cup/170 g semisweet chocolate chips

⅔ cup/105 g raisins

COOKIES AROUND THE WORLD

Although chocolate chip cookies are wildly popular in the United States, they are a predominantly American phenomenon. Here are some of the cookies favored in other countries.

AUSTRALIA AND NEW ZEALAND: **Anzac biscuits**

Anzac biscuits are oat cookies made with coconut, golden syrup (a form of treacle, a sweet syrup made from cane molasses), and a small amount of flour. First made during World War I by army wives who sent them to their husbands abroad, their name (Anzac) is an acronym for "Australian and New Zealand Army Corps."

GERMANY, DENMARK, AND HOLLAND: **Pfeffernüsse**

Pfeffernüsse are small round spice and nut cookies that are particularly popular around the winter holidays. Translated literally, *pfeffernüsse* means "pepper nuts."

IRAN: **Nan-e Berenji**

Nan-e berenji are cookies made from rice flour that is spiced with cardamom and sweetened with rosewater syrup.

ISRAEL: **Hamantaschen**

Hamantaschen are triangular cookies with a sweet filling usually made from poppy seeds, prunes, or apricots. They are traditionally baked in the springtime to celebrate the holiday of Purim.

LATVIA: **Tokorzvarhitjas**

Tokorzvarhitjas, also known as bowknots, are cookies made from a sour cream dough that's rolled out, cut, formed into flattened knots, deep-fried, and sprinkled with powdered sugar.

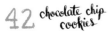

NORWAY: **Krumkakes**
Krumkakes are cone-shaped waffle cookies made of flour, eggs, butter, sugar, cream, and vanilla or spices. They can be eaten plain or filled with cream or ice cream.

PAKISTAN: **Nan khatai**
Nan khatai is an eggless shortbread cookie made with chickpea and semolina flours and spices.

PERU, ARGENTINA, AND CHILE: **Alfajores**
Alfajores are crumbly cookies made from honey, nuts, flour, breadcrumbs, sugar, and spices. They are often eaten as sandwich cookies, with dulce de leche, mousse, or jam as the filling, and may be coated in powdered sugar or chocolate.

PUERTO RICO: **Mantecaditos**
Mantecaditos are almond-flavored cookies made with flour, butter, and white sugar. They are a traditional Puerto Rican Christmas treat.

SOUTH AFRICA: **Soetkoekies**
Soetkoekies are thin, crispy cookies flavored with wine or sherry and spices such as cinnamon, ginger, nutmeg, and cloves.

SWEDEN: **Pepparkakor**
Pepparkakor are crispy, spicy ginger cookies. The dough is rolled out and cut into shapes—often hearts, but around the winter holidays the shapes of pigs and goats are also common.

GRANOLA & CHOCOLATE

MAKES ABOUT 26 COOKIES

1¼ cups/155 g unbleached all-purpose flour

½ tsp baking soda

1 tsp salt

5 tbsp/70 g unsalted butter, at room temperature

¼ cup/50 g granulated sugar

¾ cup/150 g packed dark brown sugar

1 egg

1 tsp pure vanilla extract

⅔ cup/115 g semisweet chocolate chips

2 cups/200 g granola (facing page)

Carey's mom eats granola for breakfast each day and usually adds a spoonful of what she calls "breakfast chocolate" to the mix (it's really just mini chocolate chips). So when developing recipes for this book, we came up with this recipe, which includes both granola and chocolate. We're really picky about granola, so we make our own from scratch. The recipe included here may make a bit more than you need for the cookies, but you can enjoy it as a snack or at breakfast. Feel free to substitute your favorite store-bought granola if you like, or a different homemade version.

Preheat the oven to 350°F/180°C/gas mark 4. Adjust the racks so they divide the oven into thirds. Line two baking sheets with parchment paper.

Whisk together the flour, baking soda, and salt in a medium bowl.

In a stand mixer fitted with the paddle attachment, cream the butter and both sugars on medium speed until well blended, about 1 minute. Add the egg and vanilla and mix until completely combined. Scrape the sides of the bowl with a spatula. Add the flour mixture and mix on low speed until just combined, scraping the bowl if necessary to incorporate the dry ingredients. Add the chocolate chips and granola and mix on low speed until evenly distributed. The dough should be very chunky.

Using a small ice-cream scoop or tablespoon measure, drop well-rounded balls of dough onto the prepared baking sheets about 2 in/5 cm apart.

Bake for 13 to 15 minutes, rotating the baking sheets halfway through the baking time, just until the edges turn golden.

When cool enough to handle, transfer to wire racks to cool completely. Stored in an airtight container at room temperature, the cookies will keep for 2 to 3 days.

GRANOLA

Preheat the oven to 300°F/150°C/gas mark 2. Line a baking sheet with parchment paper or a silicone baking mat.

Stir together the oats, pecans, coconut, cherries, and flaxseeds in a medium bowl.

Melt the butter in a small saucepan on the stove or in a microwave-safe container in the microwave. Let cool until just barely warm to the touch.

Transfer the butter to a small bowl and add the maple syrup, brown sugar, salt, and cinnamon. Whisk together, then pour over the oat mixture. Using a spatula, mix until the oats and other dry ingredients are evenly coated.

Spread the mixture on the prepared baking sheet in an even layer. Bake for 30 to 40 minutes, stirring halfway through the baking time, until evenly toasted and crispy. Let cool completely. Stored in an airtight container at room temperature, the granola will keep for up to 1 week.

MAKES ABOUT 2 CUPS/200 G GRANOLA

¾ cup/60 g old-fashioned rolled oats (not instant)

6 tbsp/40 g chopped pecans

¼ cup/20 g unsweetened shredded dried coconut

3 tbsp dried sour cherries, chopped

1 tbsp flaxseeds or sesame seeds

2 tbsp unsalted butter

3 tbsp pure maple syrup

3 tbsp packed dark brown sugar

½ tsp salt

⅛ tsp ground cinnamon

COCONUT-SESAME

MAKES ABOUT 32 COOKIES

1¼ cups/155 g unbleached all-purpose flour

½ tsp baking soda

½ tsp salt

½ cup/115 g unsalted butter, at room temperature

⅔ cup/130 g granulated sugar

⅔ cup/130 g packed dark brown sugar

1 egg

½ tsp almond extract

1 cup/170 g semisweet chocolate chips

1 cup/85 g unsweetened shredded dried coconut

6 tbsp/55 g sesame seeds, toasted (toasting is optional)

This recipe was inspired by the delicate and not-too-sweet sesame seed cookies we've eaten in San Francisco's Chinatown, with coconut added for both flavor and texture and almond extract in place of vanilla. Although it's an optional step, we recommend toasting the sesame seeds before baking. It will give the cookies a depth of flavor that complements the coconut nicely. To toast, heat the seeds in a small, dry skillet, stirring or shaking frequently, until they are golden brown in spots and smell fragrant. We call for white sesame seeds in this recipe, but black sesame seeds or natural (brown, unhulled) sesame seeds would also work well.

Preheat the oven to 350°F/180°C/gas mark 4. Adjust the racks so they divide the oven into thirds. Line two baking sheets with parchment paper.

Whisk together the flour, baking soda, and salt in a medium bowl.

In a stand mixer fitted with the paddle attachment, cream the butter and both sugars on medium speed until smooth and well blended, about 1 minute. Add the egg and almond extract and mix until completely combined. Scrape the sides of the bowl with a spatula. Add the flour mixture and mix on low speed until just combined, scraping the bowl if necessary to incorporate the dry ingredients. Add the chocolate chips, coconut, and sesame seeds and mix on low speed until evenly distributed. The dough should be smooth, dense, and somewhat pliable. (This dough benefits from resting in the fridge, covered, for 12 to 24 hours before baking.)

Using a small ice-cream scoop or tablespoon measure, drop well-rounded balls of dough onto the prepared baking sheets about 2 in/5 cm apart.

Bake for 10 to 12 minutes, rotating the baking sheets halfway through the baking time, just until the edges turn golden.

When cool enough to handle, transfer to wire racks to cool completely. Stored in an airtight container at room temperature, the cookies will keep for 2 to 3 days.

HONEY-PISTACHIO

MAKES ABOUT 24 COOKIES

1 cup/125 g unbleached all-purpose flour

¼ tsp baking soda

½ tsp salt

¼ tsp ground cinnamon

⅛ tsp ground allspice

⅔ cup/75 g shelled pistachio nuts (roasted or salted is okay)

⅔ cup/75 g pecans, walnuts, or almonds

½ cup/115 g unsalted butter

⅔ cup/130 g granulated sugar

2 tbsp packed dark brown sugar

1 egg

2 tsp freshly squeezed lemon or orange juice

1 cup/170 g finely chopped milk chocolate

¼ cup/60 ml honey

As much as we like the idea of baklava, a little of its sticky, honeyed sweetness goes a long way. In this recipe, we've repurposed its distinctive ingredients—chopped nuts, honey, and spices—into a chocolate chip cookie for a taste that isn't overwhelmingly sweet. Milk chocolate complements the more assertive flavors in the cookie rather than competing with them.

After some experimentation, we found that the best way to incorporate honey into this recipe is to drizzle it on top of the cookies once they come out of the oven. As the cookies cool, they absorb the honey.

Preheat the oven to 375°F/190°C/gas mark 5. Adjust the racks so they divide the oven into thirds. Line two baking sheets with parchment paper.

Whisk together the flour, baking soda, salt, cinnamon, and allspice in a medium bowl.

In a food processor, combine the pistachios and pecans and about 2 tbsp of the flour mixture. Pulse until the nuts are finely chopped, being careful to not process them too long, which would create a paste.

Melt the butter in a small saucepan on the stove or in a microwave-safe container in the microwave. Let cool until just barely warm to the touch.

Transfer the butter to a stand mixer fitted with the paddle attachment. Add both sugars and mix on medium speed until well blended, about 1 minute. Add the egg and mix until completely combined. Add the lemon juice and mix until combined. Scrape the sides of the bowl with a spatula. Add the remaining flour mixture and mix on low speed until just combined, scraping the bowl if necessary to incorporate the dry ingredients. Add the nut mixture and chocolate and mix on low speed until evenly distributed. The dough should be soft and a little sticky, similar to the consistency of crunchy peanut butter. (This dough benefits from resting in the fridge, covered, for 12 to 24 hours before baking.)

Using a small ice-cream scoop or tablespoon measure, drop well-rounded balls of dough onto the prepared baking sheets about 2 in/5 cm apart. Dampen the palm of your hand and flatten each cookie until about ¼ in/6 mm thick.

Bake for 14 to 16 minutes, rotating the baking sheets halfway through the baking time, until evenly golden. Remove from the oven and, while the cookies are still on the baking sheets, immediately drizzle the honey over them, using about ½ tsp per cookie.

When cool enough to handle, transfer to wire racks to cool completely. Stored in an airtight container at room temperature, the cookies will keep for 2 to 3 days.

A COOKIE WITHIN A COOKIE: THE 'DECONSTRUCTED' OREO

MAKES ABOUT 24 COOKIES

21 Oreo Double Stuf cookies

⅔ cup/80 g unbleached all-purpose flour

½ tsp baking soda

½ tsp salt

5 tbsp/70 g unsalted butter, at room temperature

¼ cup/50 g packed dark brown sugar

1 egg

1 tsp pure vanilla extract

1 cup/170 g semisweet chocolate chips

Chewy

We rarely buy packaged cookies, but when it comes to Oreos, we just can't help ourselves. Would it be too over-the-top to include our favorite store-bought cookie in a chocolate chip cookie, we wondered? We had to try. We began by simply chopping up Oreos and folding them into cookie dough but were less than impressed with the results. Then we came up with the idea of deconstructing the Oreos, using their filling in place of some of the butter and sugar, and the chocolate wafers in place of some of the flour. We found that Double Stuf Oreos gave us the right ratio of filling and cookie. We then added even more Oreos into the finished dough and, of course, some chocolate chips, just to gild the lily.

One note: We highly recommend you use Oreo brand cookies—we tried other chocolate sandwich cookies and didn't like how any of the results tasted.

Preheat the oven to 350°F/180°C/gas mark 4. Adjust the racks so they divide the oven into thirds. Line two baking sheets with parchment paper.

Twist open 13 Oreos and scrape the filling into a small bowl.

In a food processor, grind the separated chocolate wafers until fine; alternatively, put them in a plastic bag and crush them with a rolling pin. Transfer to a medium bowl. Add the flour, baking soda, and salt and whisk to combine.

Chop the remaining 8 Oreos into large chunks.

Put the Oreo filling in a stand mixer fitted with the paddle attachment. Add the butter and brown sugar and mix on medium speed until smooth and well blended, about 1 minute. Add the egg and vanilla and mix until completely combined. Scrape the sides of the bowl with a spatula. Add the flour mixture and mix on low speed until just combined, scraping the bowl if necessary to incorporate the dry ingredients. Add the chocolate chips and mix on low speed until evenly distributed. Remove

cont'd

the bowl from the mixer and gently fold in the Oreo chunks with a spatula. The dough should be smooth, dense, and somewhat pliable.

Using a small ice-cream scoop or tablespoon measure, drop well-rounded balls of dough onto the prepared baking sheets about 2 in/5 cm apart.

Bake for 10 to 12 minutes, rotating the baking sheets halfway through the baking time, until the centers look dry but are still soft.

When cool enough to handle, transfer to wire racks to cool completely. Stored in an airtight container at room temperature, the cookies will keep for to 2 to 3 days.

CHOCOLATE CHIP COOKIES: THE CLEAR FAVORITE

There are many types of cookies out there, but surveys show that chocolate chip is the undisputed king, with 53 percent of Americans naming it as their favorite cookie. Here's how a few other cookies compare:

CHOCOLATE CHIP	53 percent
PEANUT BUTTER	16 percent
OATMEAL	15 percent
SUGAR OR SHORTBREAD	11 percent
OTHER	5 percent

CHAPTER 3: **Savory Sweet**

This chapter is for those who like a little salty with their sweet. Each recipe contains a savory ingredient of some kind, adding a new dimension to the standard chocolate chip cookie. While some are tried-and-true combinations, such as peanut butter and chocolate chip, others push the cookie envelope with ingredients like savory spices (pages 65 and 66), cayenne pepper (page 62), pretzels (page 60), and even bacon (page 70). You may be a bit skeptical about some of these combinations, but trust us—they're all delicious.

Peanut Butter 56

Crunchy-Cereal 57

Salty Pretzel 60

Spicy 62

Duck Fat 63

Chai 65

Shichimi Togarashi 66

Olive Oil & Sea Salt 68

Maple-Bacon 70

PEANUT BUTTER

MAKES ABOUT 26 COOKIES

1 cup/125 g unbleached
bread flour

½ tsp baking soda

1 tsp salt

¾ cup/170 g unsalted
butter, at room temperature

2 tbsp granulated sugar

⅔ cup/130 g packed dark
brown sugar

1 egg

1 cup/260 g unsweetened
salted creamy peanut
butter

½ tsp pure vanilla extract

⅔ cup/115 g semisweet
chocolate chips

Peanut butter and chocolate—surely this near-perfect pairing
needs no explanation. We tested several types of peanut butter
and ultimately decided that natural, unsweetened, salted creamy
peanut butter works best, allowing the pure flavor of the peanuts
to shine through. For the smoothest texture, we recommend using
a no-stir brand. Bread flour provides added structure to the cookie
(to counteract the high fat content of the peanut butter), and a
high proportion of brown sugar keeps the cookie from being too
dry and crumbly, as many peanut butter cookies can be.

Preheat the oven to 350°F/180°C/gas mark 4. Adjust the racks
so they divide the oven into thirds. Line two baking sheets with
parchment paper.

Whisk together the flour, baking soda, and salt in a
medium bowl.

In a stand mixer fitted with the paddle attachment,
cream the butter and both sugars on medium speed until
smooth and well blended, about 1 minute. Add the egg and
mix until completely combined. Add the peanut butter and
vanilla and mix until completely combined. Scrape the sides of
the bowl with a spatula. Add the flour mixture and mix on low
speed until just combined, scraping the bowl if necessary to
incorporate the dry ingredients. Add the chocolate chips and
mix on low speed until evenly distributed. The dough should
be smooth and creamy, similar to the consistency of frosting.
(This dough benefits from resting in the fridge, covered, for
12 to 24 hours before baking.)

Using a small ice-cream scoop or tablespoon measure,
drop well-rounded balls of dough onto the prepared baking
sheets about 2 in/5 cm apart.

Bake for 9 to 11 minutes, rotating the baking sheets halfway through the baking time, just until the edges turn golden.
Be careful not to overbake, or the cookies will be too dry.

When cool enough to handle, transfer to wire racks
to cool completely. Stored in an airtight container at room
temperature, the cookies will keep for 2 to 3 days.

CRUNCHY-CEREAL

This cookie was inspired by the forbidden sugar cereals of our childhoods. We started by creating our own version of crunchy caramelized cereal. Caramelizing cornflakes and puffed rice before they're added to the dough helps them retain their texture and also makes for amazing flavor. Caramelizing the cereal is a little bit tricky, but it's well worth the effort. You may end up with small chunks of sugar at the end of the caramelization process; just discard them before proceeding with the recipe. We included corn flour for a subtle sweetness and additional cornflakes, which are finely ground, for more texture.

Make the caramelized cereal. Line a baking sheet with a silicone baking mat or parchment paper. Put both cereals and the sugar in a skillet large enough to hold the cereal in a single layer. Put the skillet over medium heat and cook, constantly stirring gently with a heatproof spatula, until the sugar starts melting. Decrease the heat to medium-low and continue to cook, stirring constantly and coating the cereal as evenly as possible, until the sugar is evenly caramelized to a medium golden color. If, at any point during the process, some of the sugar starts to burn, briefly decrease the heat to low or turn it off completely, increasing the heat to medium-low once the darker sugar has been evenly distributed. When the cereal is uniformly coated with golden sugar syrup, turn it out onto the lined baking sheet and let cool.

Preheat the oven to 350°F/180°C/gas mark 4. Adjust the racks so they divide the oven into thirds. Line two baking sheets with parchment paper.
   In a food processor, grind the cornflakes until fine; alternatively, put them in a plastic bag and crush them with a rolling pin. Transfer to a medium bowl. Add both flours, the baking soda, and salt and whisk together.

cont'd

MAKES ABOUT 22 COOKIES

Caramelized Cereal

½ cup/15 g puffed rice cereal

½ cup/15 g cornflakes

¼ cup/50 g granulated sugar

1 cup/30 g cornflakes

½ cup/60 g unbleached bread flour

½ cup/60 g corn flour

½ tsp baking soda

½ tsp salt

½ cup/115 g unsalted butter, at room temperature

¼ cup/50 g granulated sugar

6 tbsp/75 g packed dark brown sugar

1 egg

½ tsp pure vanilla extract

⅔ cup/115 g semisweet chocolate chips

In a stand mixer fitted with the paddle attachment, cream the butter and both sugars on medium speed until smooth and well blended, about 1 minute. Add the egg and vanilla and mix until completely combined. Scrape the sides of the bowl with a spatula. Add the flour mixture and mix on low speed until just combined, scraping the bowl if necessary to incorporate the dry ingredients. Add the chocolate chips and caramelized cereal and mix on low speed until evenly distributed. The dough should be smooth, dense, and somewhat pliable.

Using a small ice-cream scoop or tablespoon measure, drop well-rounded balls of dough onto the prepared baking sheets about 2 in/5 cm apart. Dampen the palm of your hand and flatten each cookie until about ½ in/12 mm thick.

Put the baking sheets in the oven and immediately decrease the temperature to 275°F/135°C/gas mark 1. Bake for 17 to 20 minutes, rotating the baking sheets halfway through the baking time, just until the edges turn golden.

When cool enough to handle, transfer to wire racks to cool completely. Stored in an airtight container at room temperature, the cookies will keep for 2 to 3 days.

SALTY PRETZEL

MAKES ABOUT 38 COOKIES

1 cup/125 g unbleached
all-purpose flour

2 tbsp malted milk powder

½ tsp baking soda

½ tsp salt

3¾ cups/185 g mini
pretzels, sticks or twists

¾ cup/170 g unsalted
butter, at room temperature

⅔ cup/130 g granulated
sugar

⅔ cup/130 g packed dark
brown sugar

1 egg

1 cup/170 g semisweet
chocolate chips

To infuse extra pretzel goodness into this cookie, we use both chopped pretzels and pretzel "flour," made by grinding pretzels. We've also added malted milk powder to play up the sweet, malty flavor pretzels naturally have. If you like chocolate-covered pretzels, you'll love them in cookie form.

Preheat the oven to 325°F/165°C/gas mark 3. Adjust the racks so they divide the oven into thirds. Line two baking sheets with parchment paper.

Whisk together the flour, malted milk powder, baking soda, and salt in a medium bowl.

In a food processor, grind 1¾ cups/85 g of the pretzels to a fine powder. Add it to the flour mixture and whisk to combine. Either by hand or in the food processor, chop the remaining 2 cups/100 g pretzels into small pieces (about ½ in/12 mm).

In a stand mixer fitted with the paddle attachment, cream the butter and both sugars on medium speed until smooth and well blended, about 1 minute. Add the egg and mix until completely combined. Scrape the sides of the bowl with a spatula. Add the flour mixture and mix on low speed until just combined, scraping the bowl if necessary to incorporate the dry ingredients. Add the chocolate chips and pretzel pieces and mix on low speed until evenly distributed. The dough should be smooth, dense, and somewhat pliable.

Using a small ice-cream scoop or tablespoon measure, drop well-rounded balls of dough onto the prepared baking sheets about 2 in/5 cm apart.

Bake for 9 to 11 minutes, rotating the baking sheets halfway through the baking time, just until the edges turn golden.

When cool enough to handle, transfer to wire racks to cool completely. Stored in an airtight container at room temperature, the cookies will keep for 2 to 3 days.

SPICY

1 cup/125 g unbleached
all-purpose flour

¼ tsp baking soda

½ tsp salt

½ cup/115 g unsalted
butter

½ tsp ground cinnamon

½ tsp cayenne pepper

¼ tsp ground white pepper

1 cup/200 g granulated
sugar

1 egg

1 tsp pure vanilla extract

¾ cup/125 g finely chopped
semisweet chocolate (55 to
65% cocoa)

Red pepper flakes for
sprinkling (optional)

This cookie strikes the perfect balance of spicy and sweet. There's just enough heat from cayenne to make it interesting, but not so much that you can't taste the other distinctive flavors we've included: white pepper and cinnamon. We infuse melted butter with the spices to bring out their full flavor and ensure that it permeates the cookie. Vanilla enhances the overall flavor, and chopped semisweet chocolate rounds it out. Finally, a pinch of red pepper flakes on top of each cookie adds a touch more heat—and allows you to customize the heat level by adding more red pepper or omitting it, if you prefer.

Preheat the oven to 375°F/190°C/gas mark 5. Adjust the racks so they divide the oven into thirds. Line two baking sheets with parchment paper.

Whisk together the flour, baking soda, and salt in a medium bowl.

Melt the butter in a medium saucepan over medium heat. Add the cinnamon, cayenne, and white pepper and stir until the spices are fragrant. Let cool until just barely warm to the touch.

Transfer the butter mixture to a stand mixer fitted with the paddle attachment. Add the sugar and mix on medium speed until smooth and well blended, about 1 minute. Add the egg and vanilla and mix until completely combined. Scrape the sides of the bowl with a spatula. Add the flour mixture and mix on low speed just until combined, scraping the bowl if necessary to incorporate the dry ingredients. Add the chopped chocolate and mix on low speed until evenly distributed. The dough should be slightly shiny and loose.

Using a small ice-cream scoop or tablespoon measure, drop well-rounded balls of dough onto the prepared baking sheets about 2 in/5 cm apart. Dampen the palm of your hand and flatten each cookie until about ¼ in/6 mm thick. For an extra pop of spiciness, sprinkle a pinch of red pepper flakes over each cookie, if desired.

Bake for 12 to 14 minutes, rotating the baking sheets halfway through the baking time, until evenly golden.

When cool enough to handle, transfer to wire racks to cool completely. Stored in an airtight container at room temperature, the cookies will keep for 2 to 3 days.

DUCK FAT

What the . . . ? Duck fat in a cookie? This recipe is for those with adventurous palates. We figured that since french fries made with duck fat are among the most delicious foods on the planet, chocolate chip cookies made with duck fat might not be far behind. Give it a try and see if you agree—or host a blind taste test for your friends (nonvegetarians only!) and ask them to guess the secret ingredient. Don't worry about this cookie being too savory; we've included coriander and orange—seasonings that complement both sweets and poultry.

Duck fat can often be found at butcher shops or gourmet food stores, or order it online at www.dartagnan.com.

Preheat the oven to 350°F/180°C/gas mark 4. Adjust the racks so they divide the oven into thirds. Line two baking sheets with parchment paper.

Whisk together the flour, baking soda, salt, and coriander in a medium bowl, using the full ½ tsp of coriander if you're a fan of this spice.

In a stand mixer fitted with the paddle attachment, cream the butter, duck fat, and both sugars on medium speed until well blended, about 1 minute. Add the egg and mix until completely combined. Scrape the sides of the bowl with a spatula. Add the flour mixture and mix on low speed until just combined, scraping the bowl if necessary to incorporate the dry ingredients. Add the chocolate chips, almonds (if using), and orange zest and mix on low speed until evenly distributed. The dough should be smooth, pale, and on the thin side. (This dough benefits from resting in the fridge, covered, for 12 to 24 hours before baking.)

Using a small ice-cream scoop or tablespoon measure, drop well-rounded balls of dough onto the prepared baking sheets about 2 in/5 cm apart.

Bake for 12 to 14 minutes, rotating the baking sheets halfway through the baking time, until evenly golden.

When cool enough to handle, transfer to wire racks to cool completely. Stored in an airtight container at room temperature, the cookies will keep for 2 to 3 days.

MAKES ABOUT 22 COOKIES

1¼ cups/155 g unbleached all-purpose flour

¼ tsp baking soda

¼ tsp salt

¼ to ½ tsp ground coriander

¼ cup/55 g unsalted butter, at room temperature

¼ cup/55 g duck fat, at room temperature

¾ cup/150 g granulated sugar

¼ cup/50 g packed dark brown sugar

1 egg

½ cup/85 g semisweet chocolate chips

½ cup/55 g chopped almonds (optional)

2 tbsp finely grated orange zest (about 1 medium orange)

CHAI

This cookie was inspired by a chai-flavored shortbread that Robyn tasted at Teaism, a teahouse in Washington, DC, and it was a favorite among our testers. Because the cookie features traditional chai ingredients—tea, cardamom, cloves, cinnamon, ginger, and pepper—we chose to use milk chocolate chips rather than semisweet, which could overwhelm the delicate flavors of the spices.

Preheat the oven to 400°F/200°C/gas mark 6. Adjust the racks so they divide the oven into thirds. Line two baking sheets with parchment paper.

In a spice grinder or clean coffee grinder, grind the tea leaves until powdery. Whisk together the tea, flour, baking soda, salt, ginger, cardamom, cloves, cinnamon, and pepper in a medium bowl.

In a stand mixer fitted with the paddle attachment, cream the butter and both sugars on medium speed until smooth and well blended, about 1 minute. Add the egg and mix until completely combined. Scrape the sides of the bowl with a spatula. Add the flour mixture and mix on low speed until just combined, scraping the bowl if necessary to incorporate the dry ingredients. Add the chocolate chips and mix on low speed until evenly distributed. The dough should be crumbly. (This dough benefits from resting in the fridge, covered, for 12 to 24 hours before baking.)

Using a small ice-cream scoop or tablespoon measure, drop well-rounded balls of dough onto the prepared baking sheets about 2 in/5 cm apart. Dampen the palm of your hand and flatten each cookie until about ½ in/12 mm thick.

Put the baking sheets in the oven and immediately decrease the temperature to 300°F/150°C/gas mark 2. Bake for 19 to 21 minutes, rotating the baking sheets halfway through the baking time, just until the edges turn golden.

When cool enough to handle, transfer to wire racks to cool completely. Stored in an airtight container at room temperature, the cookies will keep for 2 to 3 days.

MAKES ABOUT 28 COOKIES

1¼ tsp Earl Grey tea leaves

2¼ cups/280 g unbleached all-purpose flour

½ tsp baking soda

½ tsp salt

¼ tsp ground ginger

⅛ tsp ground cardamom

⅛ tsp ground cloves

⅛ tsp ground cinnamon

Pinch of ground black pepper

½ cup/115 g unsalted butter, at room temperature

1 cup plus 2 tbsp/225 g granulated sugar

⅓ cup/65 g packed dark brown sugar

1 egg

⅔ cup/115 g milk chocolate chips

Chewy

SHICHIMI TOGARASHI

MAKES ABOUT 32 COOKIES

2 cups/255 g unbleached
all-purpose flour

6 tbsp/55 g white sesame
seeds

½ tsp baking soda

½ tsp salt

2 tsp ground ginger

½ cup/115 g unsalted
butter, at room temperature

⅔ cup/130 g granulated
sugar

⅔ cup/130 g packed dark
brown sugar

2 tbsp finely grated orange
or lemon zest

2 eggs

⅔ cup/115 g semisweet
chocolate chips

Shichimi togarashi for
sprinkling

Shichimi togarashi is a traditional Japanese seasoning. The name means "seven-flavor chili," and it traditionally contains sesame seeds (both black and white), orange peel, nori, ginger, Szechuan pepper, and red chiles, though variations with other ingredients are common. It's deeply savory, with umami notes from the nori. We love togarashi on popcorn but had a hunch it might also work in a cookie. For this recipe, we include some of shichimi togarashi's more cookie-friendly ingredients in the dough—ginger, sesame seeds, and citrus zest—and amp up the savory quotient with a sprinkling of shichimi togarashi atop the cookies. If you feel a bit skeptical, rest assured that the flavors are well-balanced, with just the right amount of sugar and chocolate chips to keep things sweet enough.

Preheat the oven to 350°F/180°C/gas mark 4. Adjust the racks so they divide the oven into thirds. Line two baking sheets with parchment paper.

Whisk together the flour, sesame seeds, baking soda, salt, and ginger in a medium bowl.

In a stand mixer fitted with the paddle attachment, cream the butter, both sugars, and the zest on medium speed until smooth and well blended, about 1 minute. Add the eggs and mix until completely combined. Scrape the sides of the bowl with a spatula. Add the flour mixture and mix on low speed until just combined, scraping the bowl if necessary to incorporate the dry ingredients. Add the chocolate chips and mix on low speed until evenly distributed. The dough should be thick but not smooth. (This dough benefits from resting in the fridge, covered, for 12 to 24 hours before baking.)

Using a small ice-cream scoop or tablespoon measure, drop well-rounded balls of dough onto the prepared baking sheets about 2 in/5 cm apart. Sprinkle a healthy pinch of the shichimi togarashi over each cookie.

Bake for 12 to 14 minutes, rotating the baking sheets halfway through the baking time, until evenly golden brown.

When cool enough to handle, transfer to wire racks to cool completely. Stored in an airtight container at room temperature, the cookies will keep for 2 to 3 days.

OLIVE OIL & SEA SALT

MAKES ABOUT 24 COOKIES

1¼ cups/155 g unbleached all-purpose flour

¼ tsp baking soda

⅛ tsp salt

¼ cup/55 g unsalted butter, at room temperature

½ cup/100 g granulated sugar

½ cup/100 g packed dark brown sugar

1 egg

¼ cup/60 ml extra-virgin olive oil

½ cup/85 g semisweet chocolate chips

Coarse sea salt, such as Maldon, or fleur de sel (see Cook's Note) for sprinkling

This cookie combines olive oil and butter for a taste that is subtle but unforgettable. Olive oil has long been a popular ingredient in European desserts, and now it's showing up in more sweet dishes elsewhere. Pastry chefs appreciate how well its underlying flavors complement sweet ingredients such as fruit. A sprinkling of coarse sea salt on top of the cookie enhances its distinctive savory nature.

Olive oils vary widely in flavor, from herbal and grassy to peppery and fruity to smooth and buttery. Experiment with different varieties to find which you prefer for different applications. In this recipe, our main recommendation is that you use an extra-virgin olive oil for its superior flavor.

Preheat the oven to 350°F/180°C/gas mark 4. Adjust the racks so they divide the oven into thirds. Line two baking sheets with parchment paper.

Whisk together the flour, baking soda, and salt in a medium bowl.

In a stand mixer fitted with the paddle attachment, cream the butter and both sugars on medium speed until smooth and well blended, about 1 minute. Add the egg and mix until completely combined. With the mixer still running, drizzle in the oil and mix until completely combined; the mixture will be very loose, like pancake batter. Scrape the sides of the bowl with a spatula. Add the flour mixture and mix on low speed until just combined, scraping the bowl if necessary to incorporate the dry ingredients. Add the chocolate chips and mix on low speed until evenly distributed. The dough should pull away cleanly from the sides of the bowl and have a slight sheen. (This dough benefits from resting in the fridge, covered, for 12 to 24 hours before baking.)

Using a small ice-cream scoop or tablespoon measure, drop well-rounded balls of dough onto the prepared baking sheets about 2 in/5 cm apart. Sprinkle a healthy pinch of sea salt over each cookie.

Bake for 11 to 13 minutes, rotating the baking sheets halfway through the baking time, just until the edges turn golden, being careful not to overbake them. The cookies should still be soft in the center but shouldn't look wet. They will be puffy but will flatten as they cool.

When cool enough to handle, transfer to wire racks to cool completely. Stored in an airtight container at room temperature, the cookies will keep for 2 to 3 days.

Cook's Note

When sprinkling salt on top of cookies, we prefer to use Maldon brand sea salt or *fleur de sel* (a coarse, hand-harvested sea salt), as both have a more delicate flavor. They also have larger grains than kosher salt, lending a distinctive crunchy texture and pop of saltiness.

MAPLE-BACON

MAKES ABOUT 30 COOKIES

Maple-Glazed Bacon

8 strips of bacon (8 to
10 oz/225 to 280 g)

2 tbsp pure maple syrup

2¼ cups/280 g unbleached
all-purpose flour

½ tsp baking soda

¾ tsp salt

½ cup/115 g unsalted butter,
at room temperature

½ cup/100 g granulated
sugar

6 tbsp/75 g packed dark
brown sugar

1 egg

6 tbsp/90 ml pure maple
syrup

1 cup/170 g semisweet
chocolate chips

Even though we know it's not the most nutritious choice, we've been known to sneak cookies for breakfast. This cookie was an attempt to legitimize that surreptitious early-morning dessert eating. Bacon and maple syrup are a classic pairing, and we were happy to discover that they also work and play well with others in a chocolate chip cookie. We don't call for any particular style of bacon—use your favorite type or experiment.

Make the maple bacon. Preheat the oven to 375°F/190°C/gas mark 5. Line a baking sheet with foil and place a wire rack on top. Lay the bacon strips on the wire rack. Using a pastry brush or a spoon, spread or drizzle half of the maple syrup evenly over the bacon, then turn the strips over and evenly coat the other side with the remaining syrup. Bake for 10 to 20 minutes, until cooked through and crisp, turning halfway through the baking time. The cooking time will depend on the thickness of the bacon. Let the bacon cool completely on the wire rack, then chop it into bite-size pieces. Set aside.

Set the oven to 350°F/180°C/gas mark 4. Adjust the racks so they divide the oven into thirds. Line two baking sheets with parchment paper.

Whisk together the flour, baking soda, and salt in a medium bowl.

In a stand mixer fitted with the paddle attachment, cream the butter and both sugars on medium speed until smooth and well blended, about 1 minute. Add the egg, and mix until completely combined. With the mixer still running, drizzle in the maple syrup and mix until completely combined. Scrape the sides of the bowl with a spatula. Add the flour mixture and mix on low speed until just combined, scraping the bowl if necessary to incorporate the dry ingredients. Add the chocolate chips and prepared bacon and mix on low speed until evenly distributed. The dough should be thick and sticky. (This dough benefits from resting in the fridge, covered, for 12 to 24 hours before baking.)

cont'd

Using a small ice-cream scoop or tablespoon measure, drop well-rounded balls of dough onto the prepared baking sheets about 2 in/5 cm apart. Dampen the palm of your hand and flatten each cookie until about ½ in/12 mm thick.

Bake for 18 to 20 minutes, rotating the baking sheets halfway through the baking time, just until the edges turn golden.

When cool enough to handle, transfer to wire racks to cool completely. Stored in an airtight container at room temperature, the cookies will keep for 2 to 3 days.

CHAPTER 4: Alternative Ingredients

We developed the cookies in this chapter for those who have allergies or dietary restrictions or who are simply interested in experimenting with healthful alternative ingredients in baking. There are many alternative flours and fats out there—but we particularly like the combinations in these recipes.

Ingredients like whole grains, sweet potatoes, and almond flour are delicious in their own right, and in these cookies we are playing up these flavors, rather than trying to cover them up or take away what makes them unique.

Buckwheat & Whole-Wheat 76

Vegan 78

Sweet Potato 79

Gluten-Free Almond Flour 80

Gluten-Free Quinoa-Millet 81

Meringue 82

BUCKWHEAT & WHOLE-WHEAT

We like the toasty, earthy taste of buckwheat, especially in crêpes and pancakes. Despite its name, buckwheat isn't even remotely related to wheat; it's the seed of a plant in the rhubarb family. It's an excellent source of fiber, all eight essential amino acids, magnesium, and many of the B vitamins. (Feeling healthy yet?) Because the flavor of buckwheat can be a little overwhelming on its own, we also include whole-wheat flour for balance.

Preheat the oven to 350°F/180°C/gas mark 4. Adjust the racks so they divide the oven into thirds. Line two baking sheets with parchment paper.

Whisk together both flours, the baking soda, and salt in a medium bowl.

In a stand mixer fitted with the paddle attachment, cream the butter and both sugars on medium speed until smooth and well blended, about 1 minute. Add the egg and mix until completely combined. Add the egg yolk and vanilla and mix until completely combined. Scrape the sides of the bowl with a spatula. Add the flour mixture and mix on low speed until just combined, scraping the bowl if necessary to incorporate the dry ingredients. Add the chocolate chips and mix on low speed until evenly distributed. The dough should be thick and stiff. (This dough benefits from resting in the fridge, covered, for 12 to 24 hours before baking.)

Using a small ice-cream scoop or tablespoon measure, drop well-rounded balls of dough onto the prepared baking sheets about 2 in/5 cm apart.

Bake for 12 to 14 minutes, rotating the baking sheets halfway through the baking time, just until the edges darken slightly and look set.

When cool enough to handle, transfer to wire racks to cool completely. Stored in an airtight container at room temperature, the cookies will keep for 2 to 3 days.

MAKES ABOUT 24 COOKIES

6 tbsp/50 g buckwheat flour

1 cup plus 2 tbsp/140 g whole-wheat flour

½ tsp baking soda

½ tsp salt

5 tbsp/70 g unsalted butter, at room temperature

⅓ cup/65 g granulated sugar

⅔ cup/130 g packed dark brown sugar

1 egg

1 egg yolk

1 tsp pure vanilla extract

1 cup/170 g semisweet chocolate chips

VEGAN

1 cup/125 g unbleached all-purpose flour

⅔ cup/80 g Kamut flour

½ tsp baking soda

½ tsp salt

⅔ cup/160 ml grapeseed oil

6 tbsp/75 g granulated sugar

6 tbsp/75 g packed dark brown sugar

¼ cup/60 ml water

1 tbsp cornstarch

1 tbsp pure vanilla extract

¼ to ½ cup/40 to 85 g semisweet chocolate chips

¼ cup/25 g chopped pecans (optional)

Neither of us is vegan. In fact, the word *vegan* when applied to baking generally sends us running in the other direction. We thought for sure we'd need to add a bunch of weird ingredients to compensate for not using butter and egg in this cookie, but we were pleasantly surprised. To make up for the flavor usually provided by butter, we chose Kamut flour, which is made from an ancient variety of wheat and has a naturally buttery taste. We used grapeseed oil because it has the most neutral flavor of all the vegetable oils. Cornstarch plus a bit of water acts as a binder, replacing the egg. However, it's important to bake this dough immediately after mixing it; otherwise it will separate.

Preheat the oven to 350°F/180°C/gas mark 4. Adjust the racks so they divide the oven into thirds. Line two baking sheets with parchment paper.

Whisk together both flours, the baking soda, and salt in a medium bowl.

Either by hand or in a stand mixer with the whip attachment, whisk together the grapeseed oil, both sugars, the water, cornstarch, and vanilla until well blended. Scrape the sides of the bowl with a spatula. Add the flour mixture and, using a spatula or the stand mixer with the paddle attachment on low speed, mix until just combined, scraping the bowl if necessary to incorporate the dry ingredients. Add the chocolate chips and pecans (using only ¼ cup of chocolate chips if using the pecans). Mix until evenly distributed. The dough should be slightly shiny.

Using a small ice-cream scoop or tablespoon measure, drop well-rounded balls of dough onto the prepared baking sheets about 2 in/5 cm apart.

Bake for 10 to 12 minutes, rotating the baking sheets halfway through the baking time, just until the edges turn golden.

When cool enough to handle, transfer to wire racks to cool completely. Stored in an airtight container at room temperature, the cookies will keep for 2 to 3 days.

SWEET POTATO

This cookie is on the cakey side, but the sweet potato keeps the texture extremely moist and light. If sweet potato seems like a strange ingredient for a cookie, just think about pumpkin pie and carrot cake—two beloved desserts. Like pumpkins and carrots, sweet potatoes have an earthy sweetness and are a nutritional powerhouse, naturally rich in vitamin A and beta-carotene. Whole-wheat flour adds even more nutrition, along with a hearty flavor that complements the sweet potato.

Preheat the oven to 400°F/200°C/gas mark 6.

 Put the sweet potato in a small baking pan, cover tightly, and bake for about 30 minutes, until fork-tender. Cool slightly and mash until smooth. Measure out ½ cup/130 g of the mashed sweet potato and set aside, reserving any remaining sweet potato for another use.

 Decrease the oven temperature to 350°F/180°C/gas mark 4. Adjust the racks so they divide the oven into thirds. Line two baking sheets with parchment paper.

 Whisk together both flours, the baking soda, salt, and nutmeg in a medium bowl.

 In a stand mixer fitted with the paddle attachment, cream the butter and both sugars on medium speed until well blended, about 1 minute. Add the mashed sweet potato and mix until completely combined. Add the egg and vanilla and mix until completely combined. Scrape the sides of the bowl with a spatula. Add the flour mixture and mix on low speed until just combined, scraping the bowl if necessary to incorporate the dry ingredients. Add the chocolate chips and pecans and mix on low speed until evenly distributed. The dough should be thick and pasty.

 Using a small ice-cream scoop or tablespoon measure, drop well-rounded balls of dough onto the prepared baking sheets about 2 in/5 cm apart.

 Bake for 12 to 14 minutes, rotating the baking sheets halfway through the baking time, just until the edges turn golden.

 When cool enough to handle, transfer to wire racks to cool completely. Stored in an airtight container at room temperature, the cookies will keep for 2 to 3 days.

MAKES ABOUT 24 COOKIES

1 medium sweet potato, peeled and chopped into 2-in/5-cm chunks

1 cup/125 g unbleached all-purpose flour

½ cup/60 g whole-wheat flour

¼ tsp baking soda

¼ tsp salt

¼ tsp freshly grated or ground nutmeg

½ cup/115 g unsalted butter, at room temperature

¼ cup/50 g granulated sugar

⅔ cup/130 g packed dark brown sugar

1 egg

½ tsp pure vanilla extract

½ cup/85 g semisweet chocolate chips

½ cup/55 g chopped pecans

Soft

GLUTEN-FREE ALMOND FLOUR

MAKES ABOUT 21 COOKIES

2 cups/240 g almond flour

½ tsp baking soda

¼ tsp salt

¼ cup/55 g unsalted butter, at room temperature

¼ cup/50 g granulated sugar

¼ cup/50 g packed dark brown sugar

1 egg

1 tsp pure vanilla extract

1 cup/170 g semisweet chocolate chips

These days, gluten-free products, cookies included, are popping up everywhere, and more and more home bakers are looking for ways to make their creations gluten-free. We're all for this, but we've also found that packaged gluten-free flour blends can often be grainy and gritty, and that some can leave a funny aftertaste. We went searching for a good alternative and found it in almond flour. Almond flour is simply ground-up blanched almonds, so it has a naturally rich, nutty taste. It's also coarser and more moist than all-purpose flour. If you need more inducement to try this recipe, almonds are high in fiber, vitamins (especially B and E), and minerals and low in carbohydrates, and can help reduce cholesterol levels.

We order almond flour from www.bobsredmill.com, but you can probably find it at your local natural food store or specialty grocers, or even a well-stocked supermarket. Store almond flour in the freezer, as it can go rancid more quickly than grain-based flours.

Preheat the oven to 350°F/180°C/gas mark 4. Adjust the racks so they divide the oven into thirds. Line two baking sheets with parchment paper.

Whisk together the almond flour, baking soda, and salt in a medium bowl.

In a stand mixer fitted with the paddle attachment, cream the butter and both sugars on medium speed until smooth and well blended, about 1 minute. Add the egg and vanilla and mix until completely combined. Scrape the sides of the bowl with a spatula. Add the flour mixture and mix on low speed until just combined, scraping the bowl if necessary to incorporate the dry ingredients. Add the chocolate chips and mix on low speed until evenly distributed. The dough should be slightly sticky.

Using a small ice-cream scoop or tablespoon measure, drop well-rounded balls of dough onto the prepared baking sheets about 2 in/5 cm apart.

Bake for 12 to 14 minutes, rotating the baking sheets halfway through the baking time, until evenly golden.

Let cool completely on the baking sheets. Stored in an airtight container at room temperature, the cookies will keep for 2 to 3 days.

GLUTEN-FREE QUINOA-MILLET

This recipe employs two alternative flours—quinoa and millet—for a completely gluten-free cookie. Millet is a cereal grain that's high in B vitamins, calcium, and iron; it has a mild taste that some people compare to unflavored popcorn. Quinoa is the seed from a plant domesticated in the Andes thousands of years ago. It's a rich source of essential amino acids. When quinoa flour is used in baked goods, it contributes a mellow, peanutty quality.

Alternative flours generally aren't as smooth as all-purpose flour, but we find that these two flours combine to make a cookie with a pleasing crunchy texture and unique flavor that provide a perfect backdrop for chocolate chips and chopped pecans.

Preheat the oven to 375°F/190°C/gas mark 5. Adjust the racks so they divide the oven into thirds. Line two baking sheets with parchment paper.

Whisk together both flours, the baking soda, and salt in a medium bowl.

Melt the butter in a small saucepan on the stove or in a microwave-safe container in the microwave. Let cool until just barely warm to the touch.

Transfer the butter to a stand mixer fitted with the paddle attachment. Add both sugars and mix on medium speed until well blended, about 1 minute. Add the egg and vanilla and mix until completely combined. Scrape the sides of the bowl with a spatula. Add the flour mixture and mix on low speed until just combined, scraping the bowl if necessary to incorporate the dry ingredients. Add the chocolate chips and pecans and mix on low speed until evenly distributed. The dough may look slightly gritty due to the alternative flours. (This dough benefits from resting in the fridge, covered, for 12 to 24 hours before baking.)

Using a small ice-cream scoop or tablespoon measure, drop well-rounded balls of dough onto the prepared baking sheets about 2 in/5 cm apart. Dampen the palm of your hand and flatten each cookie until about ¼ in/6 mm thick.

Bake for 11 to 13 minutes, rotating the baking sheets halfway through the baking time, until almost uniformly golden.

When cool enough to handle, transfer to wire racks to cool completely. The cookies will get crisper as they cool. Stored in an airtight container at room temperature, the cookies will keep for 2 to 3 days.

MAKES ABOUT 26 COOKIES

¾ cup/90 g quinoa flour

¼ cup/30 g millet flour

¼ tsp baking soda

½ tsp salt

½ cup/115 g unsalted butter

⅔ cup/130 g granulated sugar

⅓ cup/65 g packed dark brown sugar

1 egg

1 tsp pure vanilla extract

¾ cup/125 g semisweet chocolate chips

¾ cup/85 g chopped pecans

Crispy

MERINGUE

MAKES ABOUT 30 COOKIES

½ cup/100 g packed dark brown sugar

3 egg whites, at room temperature

⅛ tsp salt

¼ tsp pure vanilla extract

½ cup/85 g finely chopped semisweet chocolate (55 to 65% cocoa)

We won't go so far as to say that meringues are "healthful," but since they *are* dairy-free and gluten-free and taste incredibly light and airy, they rank fairly low on the cookie guilt scale. They take some time to make, but most of that time is for baking, not hands-on time, so you can be doing something else as long as you're able to check the oven periodically.

Flecked with finely chopped chocolate, these cookies are beautiful whether piped carefully from a pastry bag or portioned quickly with a spoon. If you use a pastry bag, we recommend a large (#8 or #9) plain tip. Just remember that they won't spread or change form during baking, so they will have the same shape when they come out of the oven as they had going in.

You'll get superior results if you bake on a day with low humidity. The goal of the long, low-temperature baking is to remove the moisture from the egg whites, and humidity will hinder that process. Also note that because older eggs contain less moisture they are actually preferable for this recipe.

Finally, this cookie dough cannot be frozen before baking, though you can freeze the cookies afterward. Stored in an airtight container, they will keep in the freezer for up to one month. Just let them thaw to room temperature for 5 to 10 minutes before eating.

Preheat the oven to 400°F/200°C/gas mark 6. Adjust the racks so they divide the oven into thirds. Line two baking sheets with parchment paper.

Sift the brown sugar into a small bowl, forcing it through the strainer with your fingers or a spatula if necessary.

Thoroughly clean and dry the bowl of a stand mixer. With the whip attachment, whip the egg whites on medium-low speed until frothy, 1 to 2 minutes. Then add the brown sugar gradually, approximately 2 tsp at a time, whipping until fully incorporated after each addition. Once all the sugar has been added, increase the mixer speed to high and whip until the egg whites form stiff peaks and have a satiny sheen, about 3 minutes. To test for stiff peaks, dip the whip attachment or a spoon or spatula into the egg whites, then turn it upside down. The peak that forms should stay completely upright. If it droops or drips down, continue to whip in 10- to 15-second intervals.

cont'd

Using a spatula, gently fold in the salt and vanilla, then fold in the chocolate.

Using a pastry bag, a small ice-cream scoop, or two tablespoons (use one spoon to scoop up the meringue and the other to transfer it), portion the meringue onto the prepared baking sheets. Only minimal space is needed between the meringues, as they won't expand or change shape during baking.

Put the baking sheets in the oven and immediately decrease the temperature to 200°F/95°C/gas mark ¼. Bake for 1½ to 3 hours, depending on the relative humidity, checking every 15 minutes after the first 1½ hours. To test for doneness, remove a single meringue and allow it to cool to room temperature. Meringues are fully baked when, once cooled, they look dry and aren't sticky to the touch.

Cool the meringues completely before storing. They are extremely susceptible to humidity and must be kept in a tightly sealed airtight container. Depending on humidity, meringues will keep for up to 3 days, though they may soften in as few as 12 hours.

CHOCOLATE BY THE NUMBERS

If you're a chocolate chip cookie lover, it's likely that you also love chocolate. Think you eat a lot of it? See how you stack up to the rest of the world in yearly consumption:

GERMANY	25.1 lb/11.4 kg per person
SWITZERLAND	23.8 lb/10.8 kg per person
UNITED KINGDOM	22.7 lb/10.3 kg per person
NORWAY	21.6 lb/9.8 kg per person
DENMARK	19.0 lb/8.6 kg per person
BELGIUM	15.0 lb/6.8 kg per person
AUSTRALIA	13.2 lb/6.0 kg per person
UNITED STATES	11.2 lb/5.1 kg per person
BRAZIL	5.5 lb/2.5 kg per person
JAPAN	4.9 lb/2.2 kg per person

A couple more fun morsels of chocolate trivia:

- Chocolate is an $83 billion yearly business, making its value larger than the GDP of more than 130 nations.
- Europeans eat nearly half of the chocolate produced worldwide each year.

CHAPTER 5: # Grown-Up Cookies

The cookies in this chapter are meant to impress: They're a bit more refined and sophisticated than many of the others in this book. Though they may not be traditional, they still retain the flavors and the essence of the classic chocolate chip cookie.

The addition of alcohol in a boozy bourbon cookie (page 90) gives it an obvious grown-up factor, while browning butter for a cookie (page 88) or adding espresso powder and cacao nibs to a dough (page 96) results in recipes with rich, complex flavor. And the nibby shortbread (page 97) with its pleasing square shape, would be the perfect addition to a fancy tea party.

Brown Butter 88

Boozy Bourbon 90

Salted Caramel 91

Mocha Nib 96

Nibby Shortbread 97

Macarons 100

Tuiles 103

BROWN BUTTER

MAKES ABOUT 20 COOKIES

10 tbsp/145 g unsalted butter

1½ cups/185 g unbleached all-purpose flour

½ tsp baking soda

½ tsp salt

½ cup/100 g granulated sugar

⅓ cup/65 g packed dark brown sugar

1 egg

½ tsp pure vanilla extract

⅔ cup/115 g semisweet chocolate chips

⅔ cup/75 g chopped nuts (optional)

When developing recipes, we like to keep things simple. We try to use the fewest ingredients possible to achieve the desired result, rather than add a lot of unnecessary or artificial extras. If we're looking for innovative ways to add flavor, we often experiment with basic ingredients to see if we can transform them in new and interesting ways. Sometimes the results are a disaster, but this recipe is a good example of successful experimentation. When butter is browned, it loses some of its sweet milkiness and takes on a deeper, almost nutty taste that contributes a distinctive and delicious complexity to this cookie.

Melt 8 tbsp/115 g of the butter in a small saucepan over medium-high heat. Continue heating. Foam will form on top and then subside. Once the foam subsides, decrease the heat to medium-low. In 1 to 3 minutes, the milk solids at the bottom of the pan will turn a golden-brown color and the aroma of the butter will become deeper and nutty. When the butter solids are a very deep brown, remove from the heat, add the remaining 2 tbsp butter, and whisk until melted. Transfer to a small bowl and refrigerate for about 1 hour, until it has the consistency of room-temperature butter.

Preheat the oven to 350°F/180°C/gas mark 4. Adjust the racks so they divide the oven into thirds. Line two baking sheets with parchment paper.

Whisk together the flour, baking soda, and salt in a medium bowl.

In a stand mixer fitted with the paddle attachment, cream the brown butter and both sugars on medium speed until well blended. Add the egg and vanilla and mix until completely combined. Scrape the sides of the bowl with a spatula. Add the flour mixture and mix on low speed until just combined, scraping the bowl if necessary to incorporate the dry ingredients. Add the chocolate chips and nuts (if using) and mix on low speed until evenly distributed. The dough may be slightly dry. (This dough benefits from resting in the fridge, covered, for 12 to 24 hours before baking.)

Using a small ice-cream scoop or tablespoon measure, drop well-rounded balls of dough onto the prepared baking sheets about 2 in/5 cm apart. Dampen the palm of your hand and flatten each cookie until about ½ in/12 mm thick.

Bake for 11 to 13 minutes, rotating the baking sheets halfway through the baking time, until evenly golden.

When cool enough to handle, transfer to wire racks to cool completely. Stored in an airtight container at room temperature, the cookies will keep for 2 to 3 days.

BOOZY BOURBON

MAKES ABOUT 34 COOKIES

2¼ cups/280 g unbleached
all-purpose flour

½ tsp baking soda

½ tsp salt

½ cup/115 g unsalted
butter, at room temperature

1 cup plus 2 tsp/210 g
granulated sugar

⅓ cup/65 g packed dark
brown sugar

1 egg

6 tbsp/90 ml bourbon

⅔ cup/115 g semisweet
chocolate chips

⅔ cup/75 g chopped nuts
(optional)

Why not make a boozy cookie? We're all adults here. When developing this recipe, we experimented with several different liquors and found that bourbon worked best. Often used in Southern desserts, bourbon has an inherent sweetness and often vanilla and caramel undertones, making it particularly well suited to use in baking.

Preheat the oven to 350°F/180°C/gas mark 4. Adjust the racks so they divide the oven into thirds. Line two baking sheets with parchment paper.

Whisk together the flour, baking soda, and salt in a medium bowl.

In a stand mixer fitted with the paddle attachment, cream the butter and both sugars on medium speed until smooth and well blended, about 1 minute. Add the egg and mix until completely combined. Add the bourbon gradually, approximately 1 tbsp at a time, mixing until completely incorporated after each addition. Scrape the sides of the bowl with a spatula. Add the flour mixture and mix on low speed until just combined, scraping the bowl if necessary to incorporate the dry ingredients. Add the chocolate chips and nuts (if using) and mix on low speed until evenly distributed. The dough should be smooth, dense, and somewhat pliable. (This dough benefits from resting in the fridge, covered, for 12 to 24 hours before baking.)

Using a small ice-cream scoop or tablespoon measure, drop well-rounded balls of dough onto the prepared baking sheets about 2 in/5 cm apart.

Bake for 13 to 15 minutes, rotating the baking sheets halfway through the baking time, until brown on the edges and a light tan color in the middle. These cookies will be on the pale side when baked.

When cool enough to handle, transfer to wire racks to cool completely. Stored in an airtight container at room temperature, the cookies will keep for 2 to 3 days.

SALTED CARAMEL

We love the balanced flavor of salted caramel. We wondered whether we could work it into a chocolate chip cookie and decided to aim for a cookie with a caramelly chew. Unfortunately, our early efforts were less than successful. In one batch, the caramel oozed out of the cookies and all over the baking sheet, forming one huge molten mass of caramel-cookie (not especially fun to eat, and even less fun to clean up). The next experiment produced cookies that were teeth-shatteringly crunchy. But we persisted, and our missteps eventually paved the way to a delicious cookie with just the right balance of salty caramel in a buttery cookie.

This recipe is a bit involved but, trust us, it's worth it. By the way, you'll need a candy thermometer for making the caramel.

Make the caramel. Line an 8-in/20-cm square baking pan with parchment paper and coat the parchment liberally with cooking spray. Put the granulated sugar and corn syrup in a small sauce-pan. Add the water and stir to combine; the mixture should have the consistency of wet sand. With a wet hand or pastry brush, wipe down the sides of the pan to remove any sugar granules stuck to the sides. Put the pan over high heat and cook with-out stirring (stirring will cause crystallization). Once the water has evaporated, the sugar will begin to caramelize. Once it takes on some color, stir it to evenly distribute the heat.

Continue cooking until the sugar is a dark amber color and reads about 365°F/185°C on a candy thermometer. Immediately remove from the heat and, wearing an oven mitt to protect your hand and arm from the bubbling and splatter-ing, whisk in the cream. Whisk in the butter. Put the pan over medium heat and cook, stirring constantly, until the mixture reaches the soft ball stage: 235°F to 240°F/113°C to 116°C on a candy thermometer. Remove from the heat and stir in the salt. Immediately pour the mixture into the prepared pan and refrigerate, uncovered, until it has a scoopable consistency, 30 to 45 minutes.

Preheat the oven to 350°F/180°C/gas mark 4. Adjust the racks so they divide the oven into thirds. Line two baking sheets with parchment paper.

cont'd

MAKES ABOUT 20 COOKIES

Caramel

¼ cup/50 g granulated sugar

2 tbsp light corn syrup

¼ cup water

¼ cup/60 ml heavy cream

1 tbsp unsalted butter, at room temperature

½ tsp salt

2¼ cups/280 g unbleached all-purpose flour

½ tsp baking soda

½ tsp salt

½ cup/115 g unsalted butter, at room temperature

1 cup plus 2 tbsp/225 g granulated sugar

⅓ cup/65 g packed dark brown sugar

1 egg

¼ cup/60 ml milk

½ tsp pure vanilla extract

⅔ cup/115 g semisweet chocolate chips

Whisk together the flour, baking soda, and salt in a medium bowl.

In a stand mixer fitted with the paddle attachment, cream the butter and both sugars on medium speed until smooth and well blended, about 1 minute. Add the egg and mix until completely combined. Add the milk and vanilla and mix until completely combined. Scrape the sides of the bowl with a spatula. Add the flour mixture and mix on low speed until just combined, scraping the bowl if necessary to incorporate the dry ingredients. Add the chocolate chips and mix on low speed until evenly distributed. The dough should be somewhat sticky. (This dough benefits from resting in the fridge, covered, for 12 to 24 hours before baking.)

Using a small ice-cream scoop or tablespoon measure, scoop out well-rounded balls of dough. Make a hollow in each ball of dough with your thumb, and push no more than ½ tsp of caramel into the hollow. Close the dough around the caramel, adding a bit more dough if necessary to enclose it (failing to do so may result in the aforementioned single molten caramel-cookie that fills the baking sheet). Place the filled dough on the prepared baking sheets, seam-side down, about 2 in/5 cm apart.

Bake for 12 to 14 minutes, rotating the baking sheets halfway through the baking time, until evenly golden.

When cool enough to handle, transfer to wire racks to cool completely. Stored in an airtight container at room temperature, the cookies will keep for 2 to 3 days.

Chewy

COOKIES WITH A CULT FOLLOWING

Some chocolate chip cookies are so delicious that they have their own cult following. Here are a few you might want to seek out.

JACQUES TORRES CHOCOLATE CHIP COOKIE

Jacques Torres is a proponent of resting cookie dough and also uses chocolate baking discs, resulting in an intensely flavored cookie with layers of chocolate throughout. These cookies are huge—each is made with almost 4 oz/115 g of dough!—and have a touch of sea salt on top for a savory pop. The cookies are available at Jacques Torres stores or online. The recipe is also available online.

KOROVA COOKIE, A.K.A. WORLD PEACE COOKIE

Renowned baker and cookbook author Dorie Greenspan credits Pierre Hermé with the invention of this cookie for the now-shuttered Parisian restaurant Korova, and she has included it in her own books, sometimes under the name World Peace Cookie. It's a slice-and-bake chewy chocolate shortbread cookie with brown sugar, chocolate chunks, and sea salt. The recipe can be found online and in two of Dorie's cookbooks—*Paris Sweets: Great Desserts from the City's Best Pastry Shops* and *Baking: From My Home to Yours*.

LEVAIN BAKERY CHOCOLATE CHIP WALNUT COOKIE

This cookie is large, thick, and packed with walnuts and chocolate chips. It's slightly crunchy on the outside, with a doughy, gooey middle. Order them through the Levain Bakery website, or buy them in person at Levain Bakery locations in New York.

MOMOFUKU MILK BAR COMPOST COOKIE

This sweet-salty chocolate chip cookie contains pretzels, potato chips, oats, butterscotch chips, and chocolate chips. The recipe is available in the cookbook *Momofuku* or online, and you can order the cookies online through the Momofuku website or buy them in person at one of the Momofuku Milk Bars in New York City.

NEIMAN MARCUS CHOCOLATE CHIP COOKIE

This chocolate chip cookie, which includes grated milk chocolate and ground oats, is the subject of an apocryphal story. As the urban legend goes, a customer ate this cookie at a Neiman Marcus store, loved it, and asked for the recipe. To her surprise, she later discovered that Neiman Marcus had charged her $250 for the recipe, and when they refused to reverse the charge, she began to distribute the recipe to get revenge. Although this story is untrue, the cookie is for real, and the recipe can be found (for free) online.

ORIGINAL NESTLÉ TOLL HOUSE CHOCOLATE CHIP COOKIE

We wager that this is the most-baked cookie in America—and the standard most people use for evaluating other chocolate chip cookies. This classic recipe can be found on the back of every bag of Nestlé Toll House morsels. Even if you haven't baked it yourself, you've almost undoubtedly eaten it!

Grown-Up Cookies 95

MOCHA NIB

MAKES ABOUT 22 COOKIES

¾ cup plus 2 tbsp/105 g unbleached all-purpose flour

2 tbsp plus 1 tsp instant espresso powder

2 tsp natural cocoa powder (not Dutch-process)

½ tsp baking soda

½ tsp salt

6 tbsp/85 g unsalted butter, at room temperature

½ cup/100 g granulated sugar

2 tbsp packed dark brown sugar

1 egg

1 tsp pure vanilla extract

⅔ cup/115 g chopped bittersweet chocolate (65 to 72% cocoa)

2 tbsp cacao nibs

If you're a coffee lover, this recipe is for you. Espresso powder, cocoa powder, cacao nibs, and chopped chocolate combine to make a cookie that really packs a punch.

These cookies will spread a lot during baking. Because they're so intense, you can make them in a smaller size and still get a big impact, taste-wise. If you make them even smaller than the size indicated in this recipe, decrease the baking time by a few minutes.

Preheat the oven to 350°F/180°C/gas mark 4. Adjust the racks so they divide the oven into thirds. Line two baking sheets with parchment paper.

Whisk together the flour, espresso powder, cocoa powder, baking soda, and salt in a medium bowl.

In a stand mixer fitted with the paddle attachment, cream the butter and both sugars on medium speed until smooth and well blended, about 1 minute. Add the egg and vanilla and mix until thoroughly combined. Scrape the sides of the bowl with a spatula. Add the flour mixture and mix on low speed until just combined, scraping the bowl if necessary to incorporate the dry ingredients. Add the chopped chocolate and cacao nibs and mix on low speed until evenly distributed. The dough should be slightly gritty. (This dough benefits from resting in the fridge, covered, for 12 to 24 hours before baking.)

Using a small ice-cream scoop or tablespoon measure, drop balls of dough onto the prepared baking sheets about 2 in/5 cm apart.

Bake for 10 to 12 minutes, rotating the baking sheets halfway through the baking time, until the surface of the cookies is no longer shiny.

When cool enough to handle, transfer to wire racks to cool completely. Stored in an airtight container at room temperature, the cookies will keep for 2 to 3 days.

NIBBY SHORTBREAD

Shortbread, by definition, has a high ratio of butter to other ingredients. The fat content in the butter inhibits the formation of gluten in the flour, or "shortens" the gluten, hence the cookie's name. The butter also gives shortbread its distinctive crumbly texture.

For this version, we've added whole-wheat flour, which gives the shortbread a more complex flavor, and chopped chocolate and cacao nibs for extra chocolate intensity. The result is a refined cookie that pairs well with afternoon tea or coffee.

Depending on your preference, this shortbread can be made in square pieces, as directed in the main recipe, or round discs, as explained in the slice-and-bake variation.

Whisk together both flours and the salt in a medium bowl.

In a stand mixer fitted with the paddle attachment, cream the butter and granulated sugar on medium speed until smooth and well blended, about 1 minute. Add the egg yolk and mix until completely combined. Scrape the sides of the bowl with a spatula. Add the flour mixture and mix on low speed until just combined, scraping the bowl if necessary to incorporate the dry ingredients. Add the chocolate and cacao nibs and mix on low speed until evenly distributed. The dough should be somewhat stiff. (This dough benefits from resting in the fridge, covered, for 12 to 24 hours before baking.)

Line a work surface with a large piece of plastic wrap. Turn the dough out onto the plastic wrap and form it into a rough square. Wrap in plastic wrap and chill until firm, at least 1 hour. At this point, the dough can be refrigerated for up to 24 hours.

Preheat the oven to 350°F/180°C/gas mark 4. Adjust the racks so they divide the oven into thirds. Line two baking sheets with parchment paper.

Remove the dough from the refrigerator and let it warm slightly, until easy to work with. On a lightly floured work surface, roll the dough out to a thickness just under ½ in/12 mm. To minimize scraps after cutting the dough, try to keep it in as square a shape as possible as you roll it out. Using a pizza cutter or butter knife, cut 1½-in/4-cm square cookies and place on the prepared baking sheets about 2 in/5 cm apart. Any scraps may be rerolled one time. Sprinkle the turbinado sugar evenly over the cookies, if desired.

cont'd

MAKES ABOUT 36 COOKIES

1⅓ cups/165 g unbleached all-purpose flour

½ cup/60 g whole-wheat flour

½ tsp salt

1 cup/225 g unsalted butter, at room temperature

½ cup plus 1 tbsp/110 g granulated sugar

1 egg yolk

¼ cup/40 g finely chopped bittersweet chocolate (65 to 72% cocoa)

3 tbsp cacao nibs

3 tbsp turbinado sugar (optional)

Bake for 9 to 11 minutes, rotating the baking sheets halfway through the baking time, until the edges are golden and you can lift a cookie off of the sheet without breaking it.

When cool enough to handle, transfer to wire racks to cool completely. Although these cookies taste best the day they are made, they may be stored in an airtight container for up to 2 days.

VARIATION: **Slice-and-Bake Round Shortbread Cookies:** After the dough is mixed, turn it out onto a clean work surface and divide it into two equal portions. Place each portion in the center of a 12-in/30.5-cm square sheet of parchment paper. Use your hands to gently roll each piece of dough into a cylinder with a uniform diameter, rolling it until the ends of the dough almost reach the edges of the parchment.

Move or roll one log to the middle of the parchment, then fold the end of the parchment closest to you over the log, aligning it with the top edge of the parchment. Position a straight edge, such as a ruler or bench scraper, on top of the parchment where the two ends of the parchment now meet and angle the bottom of the straight edge toward you. Slide the straight edge toward you along the parchment paper until it's wedged under the log; this should crease the parchment and pull it taut against the bottom of the log. Remove the straight edge and roll the log up in the parchment. Repeat with the second portion of dough. Chill the wrapped logs until very firm, at least 4 hours.

About 15 minutes before you remove dough from the refrigerator for slicing and baking, preheat the oven to 350°F/180°C/gas mark 4. Adjust the racks so they divide the oven into thirds. Line two baking sheets with parchment paper.

Make an egg wash by whisking together an egg yolk and 1 tbsp water in a small bowl. Remove the dough from the refrigerator and unwrap it, leaving the parchment underneath. Using a pastry brush or your hands, evenly coat the entire surface of both logs with the egg wash.

Pour the turbinado sugar evenly over both logs, then use the parchment to roll the logs back and forth until completely and evenly covered. Transfer the logs to a cutting board and use a sharp knife to cut them into slices ½ in/12 mm thick. Place on the prepared sheets about 2 in/5 cm apart.

Bake as directed.

MACARONS

Cookie

3 egg whites

¼ cup/50 g granulated sugar

1¼ cups/140 g almond flour

1½ cups/150 g powdered sugar

½ tsp salt

Filling

½ cup/100 g packed dark brown sugar

½ cup/115 g unsalted butter, at room temperature

½ cup/85 g finely chopped semisweet chocolate (55 to 65% cocoa)

¼ tsp salt

This recipe is our chocolate chip take on the classic French *macaron*. Entire books have been written about the art and science of macarons, so we won't go into too much detail here other than to say that these are petite meringue sandwich cookies, in this case with a filling made with butter, brown sugar, and chocolate. The cookies are made from almond flour, so they're naturally gluten-free.

A few macaron tips and tricks: To pipe the macarons, you'll need a pastry bag with a wide, plain tip (such as #9) or, in a pinch, a zip-top bag with one corner cut off. Piping the macarons requires a bit of practice to get it right, but even if your macarons don't look perfect, they will still taste delicious. A correctly made macaron shell will form a "foot"—a small ruffled edge on the flat side, where it makes contact with the filling, but don't worry if this doesn't happen with your first few attempts.

Macarons don't turn out well in a humid environment, so wait for a dry sunny day to make them. Also, older eggs actually work better for this recipe; because they have a better protein structure and less moisture, they make for a more stable macaron.

We highly recommend baking macarons on silicone baking mats, such as Silpat brand; they'll keep their round shape far better than if you bake them on parchment paper or another surface. Greased baking sheets will not work for this recipe.

When baking macaron shells, we've gotten the best results by nesting two baking sheets together to help disperse the heat more evenly throughout the cookies. We suggest baking just one pan of macarons (on a nested double baking sheet) at a time. Pipe one sheet's worth and pop it in the oven, and pipe the second sheet's worth while the first is baking. This means you'll need at least three baking sheets of the same size.

Finally, this cookie dough cannot be frozen before baking, though you can freeze the macaron shells after baking. Freeze the macarons (assembled or unassembled) in a single layer on a baking sheet. Once frozen, transfer to an airtight container or zip-top bag, being careful not to smash them. Stored in the freezer, they will keep for up to one month. Just let them thaw for 10 to 15 minutes before eating.

Make the cookie. Thoroughly clean and dry the bowl of a stand mixer. With the whip attachment, whip the egg whites on medium-low speed until frothy, 1 to 2 minutes. Then add granulated sugar gradually, approximately 2 tsp at a time, whipping until fully incorporated between additions. Once all the sugar has been added, increase the mixer speed to high and whip until the egg whites form stiff peaks and have a satiny sheen, about 3 minutes. To test for stiff peaks, dip the whip attachment or a spoon or spatula into the egg whites, then turn it upside down. The peak that forms should stay completely upright. If it droops or drips down, continue to whip for 10- to 15-second intervals.

In a food processor, grind the almond flour, powdered sugar, and salt as finely as possible, letting the processor run for 2 to 3 minutes. Sift twice over a sheet of parchment paper or into another bowl, discarding any bits that don't go through the sieve. Using a spatula, gently fold in one-third of the almond flour mixture into the egg whites. Repeat twice more. Fold up to ten extra times after the last addition to make sure everything is evenly incorporated.

Line two baking sheets with silicone baking mats. Gently transfer the batter into pastry bag. Pipe 28 rounds 1¼ in/3 cm in diameter onto one of the baking sheets about 1 in/2.5 cm apart. This will use about half the batter; set aside the pastry bag with the remaining batter. When the first sheet is filled, bang it on the counter five or six times. Don't be afraid to use a good amount of force. This will settle the batter and allow air bubbles to escape. Let the unbaked rounds rest at room temperature until a thin skin forms on the surface, 15 to 20 minutes.

While the rounds rest, preheat the oven to 425°F/220°C/gas mark 7. Nest the filled baking sheet inside a clean, empty sheet. Bake in the center of the oven for 5 to 6 minutes, or until you see that the foot (a small ruffled edge at the bottom) has formed. Turn the oven down to 325°F/165°C/gas mark 3, rotate the baking sheet, and bake 5 to 8 minutes longer, until golden.

cont'd

Meanwhile, pipe the remaining batter onto the second lined baking sheet, following the same procedure. When the first baking sheet comes out of the oven, increase the temperature back up to 425°F/220°C/gas mark 7, then bake the second sheet in the same way as the first. Let all the shells cool completely, then carefully peel them off the baking mats.

Meanwhile, make the filling. In a small bowl, stir together the brown sugar and butter until combined. Add the chopped chocolate and salt and stir until incorporated.

To assemble the macarons, make 28 pairs of macaron shells, pairing like size with like size. Spread a rounded 1 tsp of the filling on the flat side of half of the shells. Top each with the second shell of the pair, flat-side down. Place the macarons in an airtight container and chill for 20 minutes before serving. They may also be stored in the refrigerator for up to 3 days. Remove from the refrigerator at least 10 minutes before serving.

TUILES

Tuiles are extremely thin wafer-like cookies, often served in res-taurants as garnishes to plated desserts. While they are generally flavored simply with vanilla, we have, of course, added chopped chocolate to this version.

For the best results, make sure to chop the chocolate as finely as humanly possible; otherwise it will be difficult to spread the dough thinly and evenly enough. We find a small offset spatula to be the best tool for shaping these cookies, but a butter knife or a spoon will also work. Eat the tuiles on their own, or serve them as a garnish for ice cream.

We highly recommend using silicone baking mats, such as Silpats, when you bake these cookies, though parchment paper will also work.

Melt the butter in a small saucepan on the stove or in a microwave-safe container in the microwave. Let cool until just barely warm to the touch.

In a medium bowl, whisk together the egg whites, brown sugar, vanilla, and salt by hand until frothy, about 1 minute. While still whisking, slowly pour in the butter and whisk until completely combined.

Sift the flour and powdered sugar directly onto the egg white mixture. Whisk until completely combined. Add the chocolate and whisk until evenly distributed. The dough should be rather runny. Cover and refrigerate until the dough has thickened but is still spreadable, at least 2 hours. At this point the dough can be refrigerated for up to 2 days. (This dough benefits from resting in the fridge, covered, for 12 to 24 hours before baking.)

Preheat the oven to 350°F/180°C/gas mark 4. Adjust the racks so they divide the oven into thirds. Line two baking sheets with parchment paper or silicone baking mats.

Scoop scant 1-tbsp portions of the batter onto the pre-pared baking sheets about 5 in/12 cm apart. Spread as thinly and evenly as possible, making rounds about 2½ to 3 in/6 to 7.5 cm in diameter with about 2 in/5 cm of space between them.

cont'd

MAKES ABOUT 20 TUILES

6 tbsp/85 g unsalted butter

2 egg whites

¼ cup/50 g packed dark brown sugar

½ tsp pure vanilla extract

¼ tsp salt

6 tbsp/45 g unbleached all-purpose flour

¼ cup/20 g powdered sugar

¼ cup/40 g very finely chopped semisweet choco-late (55 to 65% cocoa)

Crispy.

Bake for 9 to 11 minutes, rotating the baking sheets halfway through the baking time, until the edges are nicely browned. For cleaner finished cookies, use a round cutter to cut a circle from the center of each tuile as soon as the cookies are removed from the oven, working quickly so they don't get brittle; if they do become brittle before you finish cutting, return them to the oven for 30 to 60 seconds.

Let cool completely on the baking sheets. If the cookies are still soft once cooled, bake for 2 to 3 minutes more, then test again.

Tuiles should be eaten the day they are made.

CHAPTER 6: Beyond Drop Cookies

This chapter takes the humble chocolate chip cookie to the next level, with recipes that use classic chocolate-chip-cookie ingredients in not-so-classic forms. A cookie cake (page 110) makes for a fun and unconventional birthday dessert, while the whoopie pies (page 114) and madeleines (page 116) blur the line between cookie and cake. No-bake (and egg-free) cookie dough (page 108) makes a delicious snack or ice cream mix-in, and a cookie baked in (and eaten out of) a cast-iron skillet (page 113) is a decadent dessert for two.

NO-BAKE COOKIE DOUGH

MAKES ABOUT 3 CUPS

¾ cup plus 2 tbsp/105 g
unbleached all-purpose
flour

½ tsp salt

7 tbsp/100 g unsalted
butter

6 tbsp/75 g granulated
sugar

6 tbsp/75 g packed dark
brown sugar

¼ tsp pure vanilla extract

½ cup/85 g semisweet
chocolate chips

½ cup/55 g chopped nuts
(optional)

We admit that we've consumed a farm's worth of raw eggs while testing doughs for this book. If you enjoy eating cookie dough but prefer to be on the safe side, or if you want egg-free cookie dough to mix into ice cream, this recipe is the answer. Just don't bake it—we gave you forty other recipes for that.

Choose a rimmed baking sheet or other pan or container with a bottom that's at least equivalent to 8 in/20 cm square—and that will fit in your freezer. Line the pan with a large piece of plastic wrap (this need not be done neatly).

Whisk together the flour and salt in a medium bowl.

Melt the butter in a medium saucepan over medium heat. Add both sugars and cook, stirring with a wooden spoon, until the sugar dissolves and the mixture is smooth and even. Remove from the heat and stir in the vanilla. Add the flour mixture and stir to combine. Let the mixture cool until just barely warm to the touch so it will not melt the chocolate. Add the chocolate chips and nuts (if using), and stir to combine. The mixture should be crumbly.

Turn the mixture out into the prepared pan and spread it to form a square or rectangle about ½ in/12 mm thick; it need not fill the pan. Fold the plastic wrap over two opposite sides and use it to gather the dough and press it together. Repeat with the other two sides. The dough should be completely wrapped at this point.

Refrigerate until firm, at least 2 hours. For use in ice cream, unwrap the dough, put it on a cutting board, and use a sharp knife to cut it into ½-in/12-mm squares. Alternatively, just eat it straight out of the fridge!

Wrapped tightly, the dough will keep in the refrigerator for up to 1 week or in the freezer for up to 1 month.

COOKIE BARS

These bars are also known as blondies. If you've never had them, just imagine a chocolate chip cookie in a brownie format, full of dense, buttery, brown sugar goodness and studded with chocolate chips. The bars on the edges of the pan will be nicely chewy, while in the center will be softer. If you like cakey cookies or are a fan of brownies, this is the recipe for you.

Preheat the oven to 350°F/180°C/gas mark 4. Position a rack in the middle of the oven. Grease a 9-by-13-in/23-by-33-cm pan liberally.

Whisk together the flour, baking powder, and salt in a medium bowl.

In a stand mixer fitted with the paddle attachment, cream the butter and both sugars on medium speed until smooth and well blended, about 1 minute. Add the egg and mix until completely combined. Add the vanilla and milk and mix until completely combined. Scrape the sides of the bowl with a spatula. Add the flour mixture and mix on low speed until just combined, scraping the bowl if necessary to incorporate the dry ingredients. Add the chocolate chips and nuts (if using) and mix on low speed until evenly distributed. The dough should be thick and pasty. (This dough benefits from resting in the fridge, covered, for 12 to 24 hours before baking.)

Transfer to the prepared pan and spread evenly with a spoon or offset spatula.

Bake for 28 to 32 minutes, rotating the pan halfway through the baking time, just until the edges turn golden and a toothpick inserted in the center comes out clean.

Let cool completely in the pan on a wire rack. Cut three times lengthwise and five times crosswise to make 24 square bars. Wrapped well in the pan or separately in an airtight container, the bars will keep for 2 to 3 days.

MAKES 24 BARS

2 cups/255 g unbleached all-purpose flour

1½ tsp baking powder

½ tsp salt

½ cup/115 g unsalted butter, at room temperature

½ cup/100 g granulated sugar

1 cup/200 g packed dark brown sugar

1 egg

1 tsp pure vanilla extract

¼ cup/60 ml milk

⅔ cup/115 g semisweet chocolate chips

⅔ cup/75 g chopped nuts (optional)

COOKIE CAKE

MAKES ONE 11-IN/28-CM ROUND
CAKE, OR TWO 8-IN/20-CM ROUND
CAKES

1 cup plus 2 tbsp/140 g
unbleached all-purpose
flour

¼ tsp baking soda

½ tsp salt

6 tbsp/85 g unsalted butter,
at room temperature

½ cup/100 g granulated
sugar

½ cup/100 g packed dark
brown sugar

1 egg

½ tsp pure vanilla extract

½ cup/85 g chocolate chips

½ cup/55 g chopped nuts
(optional)

We both have fond memories of cookie cakes from our childhood. For Robyn, this harkens back to junior high birthday celebrations in the school cafeteria, whereas Carey remembers gobbling up cookie cakes with her teammates after high school sporting events. Our palates have matured a bit since those days, so we figured it was time to update those overly sweet cakes topped with gobs of greasy, sugary frosting.

If you find yourself in need of a last-minute dessert for a birthday celebration, this is much faster to put together than a layer cake. Stick some candles in the cookie cake and—ta-da!—instant party. If you want more decoration, drizzle with your favorite chocolate sauce or spread the buttercream frosting from the whoopie pie recipe (page 114) over the top.

Preheat the oven to 350°F/180°C/gas mark 4. Position a rack in the middle of the oven. Grease one 11-in/28-cm round cake pan or two 8-in/20-cm round cake pans liberally.

Whisk together the flour, baking soda, and salt in a medium bowl.

In a stand mixer fitted with the paddle attachment, cream the butter and both sugars on medium speed until smooth and well blended, about 1 minute. Add the egg and vanilla and mix until completely combined. Scrape the sides of the bowl with a spatula. Add the flour mixture and mix on low speed until just combined, scraping the bowl if necessary to incorporate the dry ingredients. Add the chocolate chips and nuts (if using) and mix on low speed until evenly distributed. The dough should be smooth, dense, and somewhat pliable. (This dough benefits from resting in the fridge, covered, for 12 to 24 hours before baking.)

Transfer to the prepared pan(s) and spread evenly with a spoon or offset spatula. (We like to use a wet hand to do the initial spreading and finish with a kitchen tool.)

Bake for 18 to 20 minutes, rotating the pan(s) halfway through the baking time, until the top is evenly golden and the center is soft but doesn't deflate when pressed lightly.

Let cool completely in the pan(s) on a wire rack before turning out. Wrapped well and stored at room temperature, the cake(s) will keep for 2 to 3 days.

SKILLET COOKIE

Our husbands have both been integral to the writing of this book, mostly serving as willing cookie tasters when we couldn't bear to eat one more. But they also shared their opinions on what kinds of cookies should be included in the book. This recipe, suggested by Carey's husband, is based on a dessert he remembered fondly from a Chicago pub called Gaslight.

If you've never had the pleasure of eating one, a skillet cookie is an oversized cookie baked in a cast-iron skillet and served hot, right out of the oven. The outer edge of the cookie has a crackly crust, while the center remains molten and gooey. Serve topped with vanilla ice cream for a truly decadent treat.

Preheat the oven to 400°F/200°C/gas mark 6. Position a rack in the middle of the oven. Coat an 8-in/20-cm cast-iron or other ovenproof skillet with cooking spray.

Whisk together both flours, the baking soda, baking powder, and salt in a medium bowl.

In a stand mixer fitted with the paddle attachment, cream the butter and both sugars on medium-high speed until smooth, well blended, and light, 2 to 3 minutes. Add the egg white and mix until completely combined. Add the buttermilk and vanilla and mix until completely combined. Scrape the sides of the bowl with a spatula. Add the flour mixture and mix on low speed until just combined, scraping the bowl if necessary to incorporate the dry ingredients. Add the chocolate chips and nuts (if using) and mix on low speed until evenly distributed. The dough should be light in color and very smooth.

Transfer to the prepared skillet and smooth the top with a spatula.

Put the skillet in the oven and immediately decrease the temperature to 375°F/190°C/gas mark 5. Bake for 18 minutes for a very gooey center to 22 minutes for a more set center, rotating the skillet halfway through the baking time, until the surface is no longer shiny and the cookie puffs up.

Let cool for 4 to 5 minutes before digging in. Eat with spoons, directly out of the skillet!

MAKES ONE 8-IN/20-CM SKILLET COOKIE

⅓ cup/40 g unbleached all-purpose flour

⅓ cup/40 g cake flour

¼ tsp baking soda

¼ tsp baking powder

¼ tsp salt

¼ cup/55 g unsalted butter, at room temperature

⅓ cup/65 g granulated sugar

3 tbsp packed dark brown sugar

1 egg white

1 tbsp buttermilk

¼ tsp pure vanilla extract

½ cup/85 g semisweet chocolate chips

½ cup/55 g chopped nuts (optional)

WHOOPIE PIES

MAKES ABOUT 14 WHOOPIE PIES

Cookies

1½ cups/185 g unbleached all-purpose flour

½ tsp baking powder

½ tsp cream of tartar

¾ tsp salt

½ cup/115 g unsalted butter, at room temperature

¼ cup/50 g granulated sugar

½ cup/100 g packed dark brown sugar

2 eggs

1 tsp pure vanilla extract

3 tbsp buttermilk

⅔ cup/115 g semisweet chocolate chips

Buttercream

2 egg whites

½ cup/100 g packed dark brown sugar

13 tbsp/185 g unsalted butter, at room temperature

½ tsp pure vanilla extract

⅛ tsp salt

On the baked-goods spectrum, a whoopie pie falls somewhere between a cookie and a cake. It's essentially two very cakey cookies sandwiching a creamy frosting. The classic whoopie has chocolate cookies with a vanilla-marshmallow filling. Ours, of course, had to use a chocolate chip cookie, and we've chosen a simple brown sugar buttercream for the filling. These are a bit more petite than most whoopie pies, so go ahead, eat two!

Some people think making buttercream is difficult. If that applies to you, we assure you that the method here is so simple and foolproof that you can't mess it up. A final note: We don't recommend freezing this dough before baking. After the cookies are baked, it's okay to freeze them, either filled or unfilled. Stored in an airtight container, they will keep in the freezer for up to 1 month. Just let them thaw for 20 to 30 minutes before eating.

Make the cookies: Preheat the oven to 375°F/190°C/gas mark 5. Adjust the racks so they divide the oven into thirds. Line two baking sheets with parchment paper.

Put the flour, baking powder, cream of tartar, and salt in a medium bowl and stir to combine. Sift over a sheet of parchment paper or into another bowl.

In a stand mixer fitted with the paddle attachment, cream the butter and both sugars on medium-high speed until smooth and light, about 3 minutes. Turn the mixer down to medium speed and add the eggs, one at a time, being sure to mix until smooth and completely combined after each addition. Add the vanilla and mix until completely combined. Scrape the sides of the bowl with a spatula.

Add one-third of the flour mixture and mix on low speed until just combined, scraping the bowl if necessary to incorporate the dry ingredients. Add half of the buttermilk and mix on low speed until combined. Repeat, alternating additions of the flour mixture and buttermilk and ending with the final one-third of the flour mixture. Scrape the sides and bottom of the bowl with a spatula to ensure all the ingredients are fully incorporated. Add the chocolate chips and mix on low speed until evenly distributed. The dough should be light in color and in texture.

Using a small ice-cream scoop or tablespoon measure, drop well-rounded balls of dough onto the prepared baking sheets about 2 in/5 cm apart. Bake for 11 to 13 minutes, rotating the baking sheets halfway through the baking time, just until the edges turn golden. The cookies will puff up as they bake, forming small, round mounds.

When cool enough to handle, transfer to wire racks to cool completely.

Make the buttercream: Put the egg whites and brown sugar in the bowl of a stand mixer, and place the bowl over a pot of simmering water. Whisk gently but constantly until the sugar has dissolved and the mixture is completely smooth to the touch. Affix the bowl to the mixer and, using the whip attachment, whip on high speed until the mixture forms stiff peaks, has a satiny sheen, and is cool to the touch, 3 to 5 minutes. To test for stiff peaks, dip the whip attachment or a spoon or spatula into the egg whites and turn it upside down. The peak that forms should stay completely upright. If it droops or drips down, continue to whip in 10- to 15-second intervals.

With the mixer running on medium speed, add the butter gradually, in small chunks. As more butter is added, the mixture may look as though it's "breaking," or separating; this is normal and isn't a problem. Once all the butter is added, increase the mixer speed to high and beat until the mixture comes back together and looks creamy and smooth. Add the vanilla and salt and mix until completely combined. (The buttercream can be stored in an airtight container in the refrigerator for up to 1 week. Bring back to room temperature and whip again before use.)

Using a small ice-cream scoop or tablespoon measure, portion well-rounded balls of the buttercream on the flat side of half of the cookies. Top each with another cookie, flat-side down, pressing gently to spread the buttercream evenly over the entire surface.

The filled whoopie pies are best eaten the day they are assembled, but they can be stored in an airtight container in the refrigerator for up to 2 days. Or store the cookies separately in an airtight container at room temperature for up to 2 days and fill them just before serving.

MADELEINES

MAKES ABOUT 36 MADELEINES

½ cup/60 g unbleached all-purpose flour

½ cup/60 g cake flour

½ tsp baking powder

½ tsp salt

½ cup/115 g unsalted butter, at room temperature

¼ cup/50 g granulated sugar

½ cup/100 g packed dark brown sugar

4 eggs, at room temperature

2 tsp pure vanilla extract

½ cup/85 g finely chopped semisweet chocolate (55 to 65% cocoa)

Robyn's friend Katie has a two-year-old daughter whose favorite sweet treat is a madeleine. So when Katie heard about this book, the first words out of her mouth were "You should do a chocolate chip madeleine!" As luck would have it, we were looking for another cookie to round out the book, so we took her suggestion. Both Katie and her daughter give this recipe a thumbs-up. We hope you do, too.

Madeleines are small shell-shaped butter cakes, traditionally baked in small metal pans with ridged hollows. Madeleine pans typically yield twelve cakes. This recipe makes enough batter for thirty-six madeleines, so if you only have one pan and don't want to make successive batches on the same day, it is fine to store leftover batter in an airtight container in the refrigerator for later baking (it will be good for up to two days). We don't recommend freezing the batter.

Put both flours, the baking powder, and salt in a medium bowl and stir to combine. Sift twice over a sheet of parchment paper or into another bowl.

In a stand mixer fitted with the paddle attachment, cream the butter and both sugars on medium-high speed until smooth and light, about 3 minutes. Turn the mixer down to low speed and add the eggs, one at a time, being sure to mix until smooth and completely combined after each addition. The mixture will get thinner with each egg but should remain smooth. It's important not to rush this step. Add the vanilla and mix until completely combined. Scrape the sides of the bowl with a spatula.

Add the flour mixture and mix on low speed until just combined, scraping the bowl if necessary to incorporate the dry ingredients. Add the chocolate and mix on low speed until evenly distributed. The dough should be soft and light. Cover and refrigerate for 2 to 4 hours, until dough is thick and holds its shape when scooped.

Preheat the oven to 375°F/190°C/gas mark 5. Position a rack in the middle of the oven. Coat the molds of a madeleine pan with cooking spray.

cont'd

Using an ice-cream scoop or spoon, fill the molds about two-thirds full with batter. You don't need to spread the batter evenly; it will spread as it bakes. Cover the remaining batter and refrigerate until ready to use.

Bake in the center of the oven for 9 to 11 minutes, rotating the pan halfway through the baking time, until the madeleines are puffed up, light golden brown overall, and a little darker on the edges.

Immediately turn out the madeleines, inverting the pan and tapping it on the counter to release them. Wipe out the pan and let it cool completely, then bake the remaining batter in the same way. Although madeleines are best eaten the day they are made, they can be stored in an airtight container at room temperature for up to 2 days.

MANDELBROT

Mandelbrot is biscotti's lesser-known cousin—a crunchy, dry cookie historically associated with Eastern European Jews. Just like biscotti, mandelbrot typically includes almonds (the Yiddish word *mandelbrot* translates literally as "almond bread"), but it has a somewhat finer crumb and is more substantial than biscotti. These chocolate-flecked cookies are especially delicious served with a glass of milk for dunking. They also store well for a long time, so you can make a batch to enjoy throughout the week.

Preheat the oven to 350°F/180°C/gas mark 4. Position a rack in the middle of the oven. Line a baking sheet with parchment paper.

Whisk together the flour, baking soda, baking powder, and salt in a medium bowl.

In a stand mixer fitted with the paddle attachment, cream the butter and both sugars on medium speed until smooth and well blended, about 1 minute. Add the vegetable oil and mix until completely combined. Add the egg and mix until completely combined. Add the egg yolk and vanilla and mix until completely combined. Scrape the sides of the bowl with a spatula. Add the flour mixture and mix on low speed until just combined, scraping the bowl if necessary to incorporate the dry ingredients. Add the chocolate and almonds and mix on low speed until evenly distributed. The dough should be stiff and somewhat shiny.

Turn the dough out onto a clean work surface and divide into two equal portions. Shape each into a log about 2 in/5 cm in diameter and 16 in/40.5 cm long. Transfer to the prepared baking sheet, placing the logs at least 3 in/7.5 cm apart.

Bake for 19 to 21 minutes, rotating the baking sheet halfway through the baking time, just until brown around the edges but still soft in the center. Remove from the oven, turn the temperature down to 250°F/120°C/gas mark ½, and let the cookie logs cool for 20 minutes.

cont'd

MAKES ABOUT 48 COOKIES

1½ cups/185 g unbleached all-purpose flour

⅛ tsp baking soda

½ tsp baking powder

½ tsp salt

¼ cup/55 g unsalted butter, at room temperature

¼ cup/50 g granulated sugar

½ cup/100 g packed dark brown sugar

2 tbsp vegetable oil

1 egg

1 egg yolk

½ tsp pure vanilla extract

½ cup/85 g chopped semi-sweet chocolate (55 to 65% cocoa)

½ cup/55 g chopped almonds

Transfer the logs to a cutting board. Using a serrated knife, cut each into ½-in/12-mm slices. Place the cookies on the baking sheet cut-side up. They won't expand or spread, so they can be arranged tightly. Bake for 25 to 30 minutes, until the edges are firm. The cookies will get firmer as they cool.

When cool enough to handle, transfer to wire racks to cool completely. Stored in an airtight container at room temperature, the cookies will keep for up to 1 week.

ACKNOWLEDGMENTS

Over the course of writing this book we baked many hundreds of cookies, more than we could possibly eat on our own. So we're indebted to our friends and family who (without complaint, we might add) sampled our creations, provided us with feedback, and saw that not one cookie crumb went to waste.

THANKS TO:
Amy & Kader
Google's 2011 IT Residents
Karen & Jeremy
Kristen, Michele & Lawrence
Melissa & Andy
Nicci & Gibu (and first Thursdays crew)
Nikita & Ranvir (Robyn's personal Cookie Monster)
Puffer & Kelly

Rachel, Alex, Jacob & Nathan
Scott & Jen
Suzy & Chris
The Stinson Beach crew: Kathy Carey (Mom), Vin, Elaine, Frank, Kathy Tiehen, David, Tiffany, Andrea, Monica, Sofia
Walmart's eCommerce BD team

We'd especially like to thank Andrew Shaw, who tested recipes for us.

Finally, we'd like to dedicate this book to our husbands, for trying anything we put in front of them and learning the art of constructive criticism; and to Lucy, who we hope will grow up to love chocolate chip cookies as much as we do.